W9-DDH-930

DEVELOPING THE
PRACTICE OF COUNSELLING

Developing Counselling, edited by Windy Dryden, is an innovative series of books which provides counsellors and counselling trainees with practical hints and guidelines on the problems they face in the counselling process. The books assume that readers have a working knowledge of the approach in question, and, in a clear and accessible fashion show how the counsellor can more effectively translate that knowledge into everyday practice.

Books in the series include:

DEVELOPING THE
PRACTICE OF COUNSELLING

Windy Dryden and Colin Feltham

SAGE Publications
London • Thousand Oaks • New Delhi

First published 1994

SAGE Publications Ltd
6 Bonhill Street
London EC2A 4PU

SAGE Publications Inc
2455 Teller Road
Thousand Oaks, California 91320

SAGE Publications India Pvt Ltd
32, M-Block Market
Greater Kailash – I
New Delhi 110 048

British Library Cataloguing in Publication data

Dryden, Windy
  Developing the Practice of Counselling. –
  (Developing Counselling Series)
  I. Title II. Feltham, Colin III. Series
  361.323

ISBN 0–8039–8940–7
ISBN 0–8039–8941–5 (pbk)

Library of Congress catalog card number 94–065695

Typeset by Mayhew Typesetting, Rhayader, Powys
Printed in Great Britain by Biddles Ltd, Guildford, Surrey

Contents

Introduction

We have written this book in the hope that it will help both trainees and practising counsellors to examine and improve certain key areas of their work. It is assumed that you are already familiar with the fundamentals of counselling and have begun to work with clients. Rather than offering a particular method of working, this book aims to offer reminders and catalysts, each of which you may decide is more or less helpful and applicable to your own counselling style and needs. We believe that our approach here is transtheoretical and may have something to say to practitioners from any theoretical persuasion, but there may be certain items which do not fit comfortably into, or which implicitly challenge, certain therapeutic ideologies.

There are certain broad themes which we hope are evident in the book. We hope, for example, to raise the importance of explicit discussion and agreement with clients on the nature and tasks of counselling. We view this as an important area for the ethical development of counselling. This, in its turn, raises many issues concerned with attitudes towards clients. Do we take seriously their rights as consumers? Do we see them as our adult equals, entitled to be regarded as collaborators in their own personal change? Or are we inclined to see the counselling relationship as somewhat adversarial? Do we really believe that open communication between ourselves as counsellors and our clients should be overt and as free of mystification as possible? Or are we inclined to see clients as primarily unaware of their true motivations and always in need of lengthy and expert interpretation? Part of improving our practice as counsellors involves taking seriously the views of consumers and critics of counselling, and not being defensively entrenched in comfortable positions.

Perhaps the best way to use this book is first, to consider how it may impact generally on your practice, and then to focus on those areas which you think require special attention. Use of the counsellor profile (see Appendix 2) will, we hope, enable you to do this systematically. Guard against using the book to exacerbate any tendencies you may have towards dysfunctional perfectionism! Try, too, not to carry these ideas too self-consciously into your work with clients, thus compounding any problematic tendency to become a self-conscious spectator of your own counselling. We have suggested that balanced awareness of theoretical bias, and sensitivity to the many subtle needs of individual clients, is a helpful attitude. We hope this book contains a fruitful and balanced combination of challenge and support for your counselling.

Windy Dryden
Colin Feltham

Forming an Ethical and
Effective Alliance

1   Develop your use of contracts

We are well aware that the term 'contract' is repugnant to some counsellors and we too have had reservations in the past about its legalistic flavour. However, whether you prefer terms such as 'agreement' or 'understanding', you are advised to examine just how you approach the subject of communicating with clients about the work you will be undertaking together.

The term, 'contractual psychotherapy' has been used (Goldberg, 1977) to underline the view that counselling is a therapeutic partnership between informed adults which is based on explicit negotiations as to the what, how, when, where and why of their meetings. Since counselling is still in an early stage of professionalization in the UK, many counsellors may be unclear about trends which are likely to affect them in the future. We believe that clearer contracting is one such trend and, indeed, the *Code of Ethics and Practice for Counsellors* of the British Association for Counselling (BAC, 1990) contains certain clauses referring to contracting.

Explicit contracting may be viewed as significant in ethical, practical, therapeutic and (eventually) legal terms. (Although lawsuits in relation to counselling are still rare in the UK, it is wise to protect yourself by the use of accurate contracts.) Both you and the client have a right to know the limits of your responsibilities towards each other. Your communication will be more effective, and misunderstandings reduced, if initial issues have been made explicit. Goldberg (1977) suggests that by encouraging explicit negotiation you are already therapeutically engaging the client in respectful, adult assertiveness skills.

Contracts encompass all the information, written and verbal, that you transmit to clients. Because there is so much to convey, we suggest that you commit certain essential items to paper, which can be given or sent out in the form of pre-counselling information. Appendix 1 shows the kinds of headings and items you might use. Any such document must be accurate. Whether you work in private practice or for an agency, and receive fees or not, you are liable to official complaints from clients through your professional organization, if there are discrepancies between what you claim and what you deliver. The positive aspects of written material include the fact that it promotes your service, it clearly informs the potential client, it saves time within the initial sessions, and it can engender important therapeutic understanding and goals (see also Section 26). Nevertheless, the uniqueness of clients dictates that you will spend some time in the first session or sessions exploring verbally the nuances of clients' problems, hopes, anticipations and fears, and the possible limits of your ability to help in each case.

A difficulty for trainees is that they cannot always know where their limitations lie. It is an ethical requirement that you inform clients of your trainee status, yet obviously you need to do so in a manner that will inspire rather than diminish confidence. How? Perhaps a variation of the following:

> I'm currently in my second year of counsellor training at X Institute and I receive supervision from Y. Concurrently I work at Z Family Welfare Service and I have in the past worked at Q Clinic. Is there anything else you would like to know about me or my training?

Whether a trainee or not, we suggest that you invite all new clients to articulate any questions they may have about you, your training, the therapeutic methods you use or your philosophy of counselling. There may be certain information that you consider private, or your theoretical orientation may lead you to interpret such questions as being loaded with unconscious meanings. You must decide on such boundaries yourself, but do consider the perspective of the consumer. You might sensitize yourself to some of the ethical considerations involved by referring to Goldberg (1977). Goldberg has an excellent appendix (p. 237): 'Client guide to selecting a therapist and formulating a therapeutic contract'. Refer too, to Howe (1989); Mearns and Dryden (1990) and Dryden and Feltham (1992a).

Some counsellors (e.g. Stewart, 1989) distinguish between business contracts and therapeutic contracts (also known as treatment contracts). Most of the issues we have discussed here so far relate to the 'business' aspects of contracting. Therapeutic contracting refers to specific agreements on clients' goals, conceptualizations of and proposals for working towards them. (Note that contracts made between counsellors and their clients focus on the processes to be undertaken in pursuit of goals. Few, if any, counsellors or therapists commit themselves to *promises* to deliver specific results.) Therapeutic contracts, then, are arrived at after explicit agreement on which problems the client wishes to work. For example:

So you would like to focus on your avoidance of social situations, with a view to overcoming that avoidance and increasing the chances of making more friends.

Such agreements include an understanding and commitment on the part of counsellor and client. For example:

I will help you to look at possible reasons for your current behaviour and suggest ways in which you can help yourself to change. You agree to tell me as honestly as you can your thoughts and feelings and to carry out assignments we agree together.

Depending on the model of counselling you use, more detailed agreements will vary significantly. Overall, the more clearly and positively worded such agreements are, the better. See Stewart's (1989) chapter 'Making contracts for change' for an example within the transactional analysis tradition.

It is neither possible nor desirable to foresee and prescribe for every contingency. What happens, for example, if your client begins to talk about suicide, escalates alcohol consumption, becomes unemployed or experiences other stressful life events during the course of counselling? You need to be flexible enough to respond to and accommodate such contingencies, if necessary by re-emphasizing your original contract, or by making it firmer in some respects, or more relaxed. Use of the reflection process (see Section 2) will assist this process. Finally, but often most problematically, there is the question of the balance that must be struck between some clients' overt distress on presenting for counselling, and the need for initial contracting. It is not productive to cut clients off when they are talking emotionally, crying and expressing deep hurt. But it is inadvisable to allow such ventilation of feelings to displace or dilute contractual needs. In such cases, sensitively reflect on the client's distress and ask permission to raise or return to the matter of ground-rules, agreements, goals, etc. For example:

Obviously this is very upsetting for you and I don't want to interrupt, but it might help if we sorted out a few things first so that we're both free to concentrate on our work together. Do you agree?

Remember that contracts are two-way agreements, explicitly negotiated, which are likely to enhance the counselling process. You may not like or be comfortable with contracting, but a variety of studies shows that clients prefer to be given full information, to have matters explained to them and to be consulted as equals. Walker and Patten (1990) and Patten and Walker (1990) researched comparisons between counsellors' and clients' perceptions of what constituted helpful factors in couple counselling.

An outstanding finding was that clients rated 'being given explanations about counselling' much more highly than did the counsellors. Consider and implement the idea that greater clarity and less mystification about what counselling is actually improves results. Be mindful, however, not to bombard clients with information and levels of 'equality' that they do not want. Sutherland et al. (1989) found in a study of cancer patients that although a majority wanted full information on their condition, it was a very different story when it came to treatment decisions (when they preferred the doctor to 'take over'). Sutherland et al. refer to this as a potential conflict between the ethical principles of autonomy and beneficence. Holmes and Lindley (1989) speak of an 'evolving contract' between counsellor and client which is responsive to what emerges after the first few 'sample' sessions.

Key point

Consider your present style of introducing clients to counselling and what it can realistically offer. Look at the contracts you make with clients and improve those which will enhance mutual communication and facilitate collaborative therapeutic effort.

---

2 Develop and maintain the reflection process

Supervisees often report difficulties they are experiencing with clients in a well conceptualized and articulate manner. With a little reflection in supervision on the way their clients present and interact, and on how they themselves respond and perhaps feel blocked, they may readily identify core issues to explore with their clients any potential ways forward. Yet when asked, 'Have you shared these thoughts with your client?' they frequently appear surprised at the idea. Certain misconceptions about the counselling process may be responsible for this reticence on the part of counsellors.

The emphasis in much counsellor training on accurate empathy, faithfulness to the client's frame of reference, non-judgementalism and minimal questioning, appears inadvertently to foster a tendency to avoid interrupting clients at all costs. Do consider that there are, however, times when you need to create conversational space for yourself in order to introduce certain matters to the client, or to remind the client of previous agreements. We have argued that contracts need to be explicitly raised, negotiated and maintained. In the same spirit, issues to do with the ongoing process of counselling, the quality of communication between client and counsellor, and the client's view of progress, are usefully, if not essentially, aired, clarified and improved by explicit discussion.

The reflection process is what we call the process when counsellor and client agree to discuss their rational observations of the counselling process. This involves a 'stepping back' to gain perspective on the relationship and how well it is serving the interests of the client. When initial contracting has been mutually negotiated, both counsellor and client have begun to establish the foundations of this process of feedback. Certain questions may be raised by the counsellor to stimulate the reflection process. Examples of such questions are: 'Is counselling going the way you expected it to?' or 'Is there anything I am doing or not doing which is particularly helpful or unhelpful to you?' or 'I have the feeling that perhaps sometimes I am missing the point of what you are saying – is that the case?' These are direct instances of open communication, inviting the client to respond in kind.

Sometimes counsellors place too great an emphasis on unconscious and oblique processes in counselling. One argument runs that you cannot expect the client to know exactly, or without distortion, how well the process is going; or that you cannot expect certain clients (for example, those who are compliant) to be assertive enough to make negative statements. Without dismissing these possibilities, we attribute greater adult rationality to clients than those holding such positions often do. Furthermore, it is not at all unknown for practitioners to invite and respect the comments of the 'observing ego' of their clients. Strean (1959) advocates asking clients for their opinions on what they require for successful next steps in therapy. Strean's phrase 'the patient as consultant' resonates with what we mean here by the reflection process. The client is the person who experiences the impact of therapeutic interventions; therefore we need his or her view on them. The client is also the consumer, entitled to quality assurance. We suggest that the counsellor's guessing how the process is being received by the client, or making clinical assumptions based on professional experience and theoretical predictions, is unreliable.

The reflection process may be used as a means of checking on the helpfulness of arenas (the interpersonal contexts in which counselling takes place), possible referrals, therapeutic bonds, goals, tasks (the therapeutic techniques and strategies used by counsellor and client), conceptualizations, pacing and other items raised throughout this book. To check on the usefulness of a therapeutic arena, you may ask, for example:

> I have the sense that it would be very useful if you could discuss these matters directly with your wife in a counselling setting. Do you think couple counselling would benefit you?

Or about your relationship:

> It sometimes seems as if, perhaps, you are a little wary of me. I wonder if this is true, and if so, can we understand that more?

Or concerning your conceptualization of the client's problem:

> When we first discussed things, you agreed that depression was your biggest problem and that it might help to look closely at the negative thoughts you have. But now I wonder if anxiety is not more of an issue, and perhaps it might help more if we considered what actions you could take to confront and explore it?

There is very little that cannot be raised in this way. It may occur to you to use the reflection process particularly when you sense that there are important issues, perhaps not yet made explicit between you and the client, which require open, honest and accurate dialogue. It is not (please note) a process of anxiously checking out with your client every five minutes if you are 'getting it right'! Use the reflection process judiciously, and consider using it both informally and more formally at the time of any scheduled review sessions (see Section 6).

Finally, if such a climate is cultivated from the beginning, then the counsellor's observations and requests for feedback will not seem to come 'out of the blue'. When the counselling process is carefully tended in the sense of maintaining awareness of bonds, goals and tasks, then, we believe, any backlog or subversive current of misunderstanding or unconscious conflict is likely to be minimized.

> **Key point**
>
> Establish the reflection process early on and use it throughout the counselling process as a means of raising and clarifying significant issues with clients.

3   Identify and use the most helpful arena for each client

Therapeutic arenas (sometimes called 'arrangements') are constituted by 'the interpersonal context in which therapy takes place' (Dryden, 1989). The most commonly used arenas are individual, couple, group and family therapy or counselling. Individual counselling is by far the most widely used, but the other arenas are clinically and theoretically well developed. Trainee individual counsellors may have little or no familiarity with other arenas and may assume that these have little or no significance for their clients. Our intention here is to alert you to the salient issues in using or referring to therapeutic arenas other than individual counselling.

If you are working in an organization, it may be that a decision has already been made by someone carrying out an initial assessment of your clients that these clients need the individual counselling that you offer. We suggest, however, that in each case referred to you, you make your own judgement as to what may be the most helpful arena for a particular client. In listening to the concerns your clients first present, attune yourself to prominent and recurring themes, especially where these involve significant others in clients' lives. Consider which of the arenas (and there may be more than one) that your clients might benefit from *at this time in their lives*. We know a woman who after years of social work intervention, including family therapy, finally managed to break away from being perceived as simply a part of a 'problem family', secured individual counselling for herself and began later in life to flourish.

Individual counselling

One-to-one counselling offers the most contained form of confidentiality. Clients with particular concerns about confidentiality, therefore, are likely to need this arena, at least in the first instance. Particularly vulnerable clients who need to build a trusting relationship slowly, also clearly need an individual counselling relationship. Individual counselling offers the opportunity for therapeutic intimacy (the 'corrective emotional experience'), and for exclusive attention. Clearly, it offers greater opportunity than other arenas for extended, in-depth intrapsychic exploration. Clients who have been abused, who have had difficulties separating themselves from others, who need to be able to move at their own pace and disclose painful material in their own time, are prime candidates for individual counselling. Clients who temporarily cannot manage the demands of other people (such as the very depressed or highly anxious) also commend themselves for referral to this arena.

You may have to think hard about whether to offer individual counselling to certain clients. Those who may become extremely, counterproductively dependent on you as their only helper, may be better helped in other arenas. It is thought by some counsellors working with people who have serious drinking or drug problems that their inclination towards dependence on and manipulation of individual counsellors is a contra-indication for this arena. You may wish to think twice about certain so-called 'borderline', highly disturbed and seductive clients. They may represent an 'interesting challenge' and certainly some counsellors have exceptional skills in working with them, but consider the possible advantages of group rather than individual therapy, or referral to specialist individual therapists, in such cases. By the same token, clients who are skilled intellectualizers and gameplayers may benefit more from the challenges of counselling within groups. You may decide, after such considerations, to proceed to work with such clients in the arena of individual counselling; all we advocate here is that you do not necessarily do so automatically and that it can be helpful to question any tendency you have to accept *all* referrals for individual counselling.

Couple counselling

It is not unusual for an individual to use counselling sessions almost exclusively for complaining about the behaviour of a partner. Where this is apparent, it certainly indicates that the relationship is the focal problem and that the preferred arena would be couple counselling. Gurman and Kniskern (1978) demonstrated that participation of both partners in counselling significantly improves the prospects for a successful outcome. Unfortunately, it is often the case that one partner does not wish to participate in counselling. Even so, it seems apparent that a focus on the relationship rather than solely on one partner's intrapsychic concerns, enhances the prospects for a successful outcome to couple problems. (When one partner has pronounced intrapsychic problems, however, couple counselling may not be the best arena, at least until those problems are addressed with some success.) Faced with an individual client, then, whose concerns are primarily related to his or her partner, openly discuss the question of involving that partner in couple counselling with you if you have the requisite skills and the referral is a relatively new one, or explicitly discuss the suitability of a referral to an alternative couple counselling facility.

Such referrals are not always easy, however. One partner may not cooperate. There may be a long waiting list for alternative arrangements. Additionally, there are instances when, although the problem is clearly relationship-based, one partner may be experiencing abuse and threat or may wish to discuss highly sensitive material confidentially when the other is not present. Your client may have urgent need of support in making a decision to leave a violent husband and enter a refuge, for example. This is a point at which to consider the evolving contract. You may agree to a number of sessions of individual counselling and then, using the reflection process, suggest to your client that she may need to consider further individual work with you, couple counselling (with you, if you have the necessary skills or with another counsellor), referral to a refuge, or other possibilities. Also bear in mind that relationship problems can apply to both heterosexual and homosexual clients. In our experience, two key factors in deciding whether or not couple counselling is the most helpful arena concern first, the extent to which the client emphasizes the role of current relationship difficulties with a significant other in his or her problems (as compared with individual 'intrapsychic' difficulties), and second, the willingness of the other person to be involved in a couple counselling contract. The more the client emphasizes a current relationship problem and the more willing the significant other is to be involved in couple counselling, the stronger is the indication that this is the arena of choice.

Family therapy

Like couple counselling, family therapy is based on the premise that the client's problem is best viewed as essentially part of a relationship system. Bennun explains the contrast between individual and family therapy:

> The contrast between the two approaches extends beyond the participants in the therapy situation (system) and differs in the formulation of the presenting problems and the mechanisms of change. A fundamental premise within systems theory is that the problems that bring individuals into treatment persist only if they are maintained by the ongoing current behaviour of the patient and others with whom he or she interacts. If the problem-maintaining behaviour configuration can be altered, the nature of the problem too will change. (1988: 5)

The key here is to recognize when your clients' problems are being maintained by the family system of which he or she is a part. If a client makes frequent references to family members and is actively involved with them, the possibility exists that whatever advances are made in individual counselling might easily be undone by the negative influence exerted by the family system.

You may have family therapy particularly in mind if you are working with children or adolescents. But there are adults who appear to be the 'presenting client' of a dysfunctional family, and sometimes two or more family members may request counselling, either simultaneously or sequentially. When other family members are repeatedly implicated in your clients' problems, consider the possibility of referral for family therapy. Some authorities claim that family therapy is the arena of choice for specific problems. Thus, Worden (1991) recommends family therapy for many cases of problematic bereavement, particularly when the deceased was a family member on whom others relied heavily. Also, it is often thought that the treatment of anorexia nervosa is best done within a family context.

In discussing the possibility of this arena with your client, consider possible disadvantages. Your client may need the safety and confidentiality of individual counselling, even if family therapy might ultimately or theoretically be the more potent change agent. Some Adlerians claim that 'all therapy is family therapy' – that is, that the client's family are always in some way implicated – but we consider that this is not necessarily the case. Consider, too, the observations of Howe (1989) whose research interviews with consumers of family therapy indicated that they often felt that they had been given no choice of treatment approaches, and that practitioners – who were often perceived as far too role-bound – failed to explain to them what was expected of them in therapy, which was often perceived as 'weird'.

Group therapy

The main rationale for group therapy is that it provides direct help for those clients whose problems have an interpersonal focus, for example difficulties in forming or maintaining relationships. We have already noted that problems of alcoholism and addiction may in certain cases be best treated in group (including residential) treatment approaches and there are many known advantages of the group therapy arena (see Bloch, 1990). Generally, it is well recognized that the helpful factors in group therapy include: cohesiveness (members find acceptance in and a sense of belonging with each other); insight from interpersonal exploration and observation; universality (members learn that others suffer as they do); hope; altruism; catharsis; and learning problem-solving from the problems (and solutions) of others.

You may become aware that, although your client has made significant progress in individual counselling, a different kind of opportunity is needed to explore social anxieties in relative safety. Or you may have a client who is highly motivated for the kind of personal and emotional growth process that can be fostered by the more humanistic groups (such as Gestalt, psychodrama and encounter groups). Some counsellors find it both economical and beneficial for some of their clients to join together in a group, both to explore interactions and to generalize their learning from individual counselling. In primal therapy, individual and group approaches are used in combination, clients being encouraged to use the large group for risk-taking, the consequences of which can then be explored in greater depth in individual work.

Group therapy can be useful for certain clients who cannot trust individual counsellors, as well as for those whose problems are shared by many others (for example, people with eating problems, people with drinking problems, people who wish to learn assertive behaviour). Group therapy is naturally contra-indicated, however, for clients who will use groups to hide themselves, or for those whose anxiety, depression or other problems are too severe to withstand group pressures.

Remember that an alternative arena may be more helpful than the one you are offering, or it may be useful in conjunction with what you have to offer. There can be a natural progression from individual to group counselling, for example, or an interweaving of approaches according to the kind of material surfacing for a client at any one time. Budman and Gurman (1988), for example, consider it useful in brief therapy to involve partners and family members temporarily, at critical stages in the counselling process. If you have training and/or experience in more than one arena, you may find it fruitful to do likewise. It is more likely, however, that you provide one kind of counselling (probably individual) and that you will need to first, consider any unexamined prejudices you may have in respect to the legitimacy and efficacy of other arenas; second, familiarize yourself with clinical and theoretical rationales for referring to other arenas; and third, identify local or national resources, and practitioners, who provide such alternative approaches.

Key point

Do not simply use the arena with which you are most comfortable or familiar, but consider which is likely to suit each client, even if this means that you may have to refer on.

---

4 Use referral in your clients' best interests

It is our observation that some counsellors attempt to work with every client who comes their way. This is understandable if you are a trainee with little experience of who *not* to work with, if you sincerely believe that your theoretical orientation suits and can help everyone, or if you need to build a private practice. However, while it is understandable, we suggest that you consider, with each of your new clients, whether you are the best counsellor for them.

Perhaps in some ways many trainees receive confusing modelling from their tutors, supervisors and managers. Many counselling agencies, for example, have a policy of allocating clients to counsellors randomly, regardless of the client and the nature and severity of the client's problems. The policy of throwing trainee counsellors 'in at the deep end' may give many the impression that they should be able to cope with any problem. This, we believe, is not in clients' best interests. Pitts (1992) notes that many trainee counsellors in the USA are rated, among other developing skills, on their 'appropriate referral skills'. Lazarus (in Dryden, 1991a) urges counsellors to 'know your limitations, and other clinicians' strengths'. We have already discussed the use of alternative arenas. Here, we extend that principle to other areas in which your skills and knowledge may not provide the optimal resource for certain clients.

Let us make it clear that we do not wish to foster professional low self-esteem. Think of developing your referral skills as a positive enhancement of your overall practice. Lazarus, a therapist of considerable experience and standing, uses referral (which he considers a 'technique' in its own right) for a variety of reasons, not least of which is the recognition of his own non-omnipotence. He talks about seeking a second opinion in especially difficult cases, in much the same way that GPs responsibly seek specialist opinions outside their own expertise. But he is also alert to possible obstacles between himself and clients, such as differences in gender, race, language, age and temperament. By using both the reflection process and your own observations, you will become aware of those areas of practice in which you may not be appropriately qualified, skilful, experienced, or optimally suited to particular clients' temperaments.

Consider various areas of specialist counselling that may be outside your expertise. Do you have experience in working with clients with serious mental health problems or learning difficulties; with adults who have been abused as children; with alcoholic or drug-addicted clients; with men who are violent towards women; with people who are undergoing post-traumatic stress disorder; with gay and lesbian clients; with clients who have physical disabilities; with people who have serious financial difficulties? (The list could be extended indefinitely.) You may indeed have some experience, or you may be willing to 'have a go'. It is often the case, too, especially during training or soon thereafter, that you are keen to take on clients whose problems are outside your experience precisely in order to develop your skills. If you take this approach, be especially mindful of the need for close supervision. In addition, remind yourself of the ethical dimension involved, which is well put by VandeCreek and Harrar:

> Even when a client gives informed consent to receive treatment from a trainee, the client does not thereby consent to receive substandard care.

> ... A general rule of thumb for supervisors in the mental health field
> should be that the level of care provided by the trainee, with the
> supervisor's assistance, should not fall below a professional level.
> (1988: 14)

This statement implies, not that you should avoid clients who will
be especially challenging for you, but that counsellors be reminded
to steer a careful ethical course, especially when they are aware
that certain clients may tax their skills.

The need for referring on, or the wisdom of doing so, applies not
only to trainees, but to any practitioner, however seasoned. When
you become aware that what you have to offer the client is either
problematic (for example, because of your race or gender) or
possibly less beneficial than a colleague might offer (for example, a
colleague with special experience of counselling holocaust
survivors or people with eating problems), then you must
conscientiously decide whether such considerations outweigh your
own wishes. Equally, it is sometimes the case that a client will
worsen during counselling and require hospitalization or other
treatment. This may be in addition to the counselling you are
offering. Whatever the circumstances, you are faced with a need to
initiate discussion of such referrals sensitively, conveying a
message not of rejection but of helping the client to secure the best
possible help for him- or herself.

Let us take the devil's advocate position here and imagine a
client whom you perceive as requiring a kind of support that you
are not best placed to offer. He has been diagnosed elsewhere as
being 'mildly autistic' and you have little or no knowledge of
autism. Although you do not wish to reject him or to increase any
sense of stigma he already has, it is your best judgement that a
local social services facility which you know has greater expertise
and resources than you can offer. He may be gravitating towards
you as someone who he believes can magically relieve him of his
problems, his low self-esteem and his loneliness. Some counsellors
might take him on, with or without specialist skills or knowledge,
but you do not feel comfortable in that position. How will you
refer him on? Consider the following dialogue:

You: I can see that you are very keen to come here. I would like to be
able to help you. But I happen to know that there's someone who works
at the Smith Street Centre who has a lot more experience with the kinds
of issues you've raised than I have. What I'd like to do is to call her,
with your permission, and see if she can help. Or you may like to call
her yourself. What do you think about that idea?

Client: I know that place. Everyone there is weird. I don't want to go
there. I like coming to see you.

Here, of course, is a scenario in which your best judgement and the client's wishes are at odds with each other. Most referrals are not likely to be so difficult, but considering this example may nevertheless be instructive. How will you proceed? Perhaps:

You: I'm glad that you like coming here to see me and I would like to be able to help you. If you know the Centre already and you don't like the idea of going there, perhaps you can tell me some more about your reactions to it. But there are other services I know which you may prefer. What I'm trying to say is that you're welcome to come here a little longer, but in the long run I don't think I'm the best person to help you, and I'd like to help you find someone who's going to really know how to help.

This is a difficult dialogue. In certain cases, perhaps like this, it may be that all your best efforts to make a sensitive referral will be interpreted as rejection; there may even be instances when you are persuaded by the client to change your mind. You must learn where to draw the line firmly and sensitively. In many cases, however, your client will have a greater investment in finding the best form of help than in fastening on you as his or her sole hope.

Key point

Give thought as to whether there may be an alternative form of help for clients that might be preferable to what you can offer. If so, refer the client to that source sensitively and in a way that engenders hope.

---

5 Develop, maintain and vary your therapeutic bond

All counsellors are familiar with the core conditions of acceptance, empathy and genuineness, which are widely agreed to provide (usually) an optimal climate for therapeutic growth. Therapeutic bonds are, however, developed, sustained and threatened by many other factors both within and beyond the awareness and control of the counsellor. Try as you might with some clients to foster the core conditions, it may be that your gender, race, class, age or physical characteristics present an obstacle to a 'good enough' bond forming. In cases where you sense the possibility of such obstacles, tentatively use the reflection process to identify their existence and either to work through them or, if need be, to discuss referral.

There is another set of factors affecting the therapeutic bond, namely the personality differences between one client and another and the potentially exacting demands on the counsellor for subtly varying responses. It has been observed (Brazelton and Cramer, 1991) that individual differences are present and highly significant from the moment of birth. Such differences are evident, for example, in levels of robustness, activity, self-containment and demandingness. Brazelton and Cramer suggest that those parents fare better who are intuitively able to adjust their responses to the individuality of each of their babies. Similarly in counselling, to the extent that nurturance and rapport are important, counsellors who can detect and adapt to the key individual differences and interactional needs of each client, are likely to enjoy greater success than counsellors who are attached to one way of interacting.

Howard et al. (1987) put forward a compelling case for counsellors needing to adapt their manner of relating to clients, which concurs with Lazarus's notion of the 'authentic chameleon'. Without compromising the genuineness, or congruence, that is regarded as so central to the therapeutic enterprise, it is yet possible and advisable to note the cues of different clients as to the kind of relationship styles they prefer in others. Where it is apparent that a client wishes to be helped by an expert, it can be advantageous if you bring your expertness more to the fore; or where attractiveness, for example, is clearly more highly valued by a client, you may allow your informality, friendliness or humour to predominate. Sensitize yourself to such preferences, which can often be understood in terms of bipolar orientations. Does the client seem more comfortable with or more motivated by your self-disclosure or neutrality; by a high level of counsellor activity or a more reflective stance; by a more facilitative or didactic approach? We do not suggest that you swing to extremes of attempted complementarity, but that you allow facets of your own personality to become foreground or background as appropriate. In this way you are likely to be able to reach and sustain a helping relationship with a greater range of clients. A cautionary note here, however, is that you need to avoid undermining the client's autonomy or reinforcing preferences for unhealthy relationship styles (see Section 20, and especially the concept of 'cyclical psychodynamics').

Adapting to your clients requires considerable flexibility on your part. We have known students for whom it is very important that their casual dress, for example, reflects their relaxed or liberal attitudes to life. While this may be attractive to certain clients, and of no great consequence to others, it will probably be off-putting to some clients. It can be important, therefore, that you present yourself in such a way that you are free to highlight or play down such aspects of your personality. Another way of thinking about this, in terms familiar to some humanistic counsellors, is that different clients may resonate with different subpersonalities within you, which you can choose consciously to 'activate' in order to understand and help the client better (see Rowan, 1990).

If you are a trainee it is not so easy to promote your expertness, especially since it is an ethical requirement that you disclose your qualifications honestly. But you can exploit the positive attributes of your trainee status, such as your enthusiasm and openness to ideas. You can also disclose, if useful, any personal and professional attributes from outside counselling, such as your having mothered four children, having worked in a residential home, or being a retired GP. It is obviously better if such disclosures are non-defensive and are offered genuinely in order to assuage any doubts or anxieties clients may have.

Lazarus (in Dryden, 1991a) is critical of what he views as Rogers's invariably warm relational style with every client. As Lazarus puts it, Rogers 'was always the same, constantly offering his carefully cultivated warmth, genuineness and empathy to all his clients' (1991a: 18). In Lazarus's view, some clients do not want or benefit from this at all, but are better helped by other styles of counsellor-relatedness, for example, one that is more businesslike and distant. Lazarus suggests further that you can find out the kind of style preferred by simply asking clients. For example:

> I get the feeling that you are used to, and perhaps prefer, looking at your problems in quite a brisk and no-nonsense way, with someone who is prepared to confront you hard when necessary. Is that accurate?

Or:

> You appear to be very sensitive to discussing issues to do with depression, and I wonder if the fact that I can have a rather forceful manner inhibits you. Would it help if I were more easy-going and gentle?

Obviously clients may not always feel able to respond directly or assertively to such questions, but an astute counsellor can pick up cues from the way they are answered or avoided, and use this information either to adjust the pace, manner or strategy, or perhaps to return to discussion of possible referrals later. Another way of putting such requests for information is to lead with self-disclosure, for example:

> I'm aware that I'm inclined to ask rather a lot of questions and to quicken the pace of counselling. It would be useful to me if you could comment on how helpful or otherwise that is for you.

While we are advocating in this book an explicit reflection process, we acknowledge that some clients may prefer a rather remote or apparently neutral counsellor who does not ask such questions. If you detect such a preference in certain clients, then by all means adapt accordingly. If you can learn *when* certain relational styles are useful to *which clients* at *which stages* in the counselling process, then such intelligent variations will serve you well. But bear in mind too that your consistency will be very important for some clients, and do not change your approach and your manner simply for the sake of it. Remember that there are limits to anyone's interpersonal flexibility and that whenever you are exercising variations in your style, you need to do so congruently.

Key point

Be conscious of how helpful or otherwise your style of relating is for each client and be ready to modify it in the light of clients' feedback.

---

6   Consider using formal review sessions

The reflection process is characterized by your asking certain pertinent questions of the client from time to time which invite feedback on the counselling relationship and on progress towards goals. What you may consider in addition to this is the formal evaluation of your work together in designated review sessions. If your work is time-limited (for example, a maximum of six sessions), then you may be disinclined to devote a whole session or sessions to reviewing work. Even in such a short counselling contract, however, you might decide to spend 15 or 20 minutes in the third or fourth session on reviewing progress so far and on looking at remaining aims. We will assume here that you are counselling over a period of several weeks or months and that time is available for review sessions. A fairly common pattern, for example, is to arrange for an initial series of six sessions at the end of which a review is held before deciding on whether to proceed with counselling. In this instance, the first six sessions may have been agreed on as a kind of 'trial therapy', or sample of counselling.

Many practitioners prefer to engage immediately in therapeutic work without extensive assessments or explanations (see Mahrer, 1989; Davanloo, 1990). One advantage of such an approach is that it offers clients a taste of the way you work and of what counselling is. An advantage for you is that it offers you an example of your client's way of presenting concerns, a view of any possible defence mechanisms and his or her way of construing problems. For both you and the client, then, the first few sessions may be a kind of 'practice run'. If you have agreed to four or six initial sessions, for example, then you may use this experience to reflect on how well you may be likely to work together. But do negotiate this with clients at the outset. 'Would you agree to meeting with me for six sessions, and to taking time in the sixth session to discuss how helpful you think counselling may be for you?' is the kind of invitation you might issue at the very beginning. Explain to the client that it can often take time to appreciate how counselling works, and elicit the client's commitment to counselling for at least the first six sessions. If your contract with the client has been clearly goal-oriented, you may even have initiated a written statement of goals, which can then be used to refer back to at the review stage (see Sutton, 1989).

Having worked on hearing the client's general narrative and specific problem areas, and having demonstrated to the client how your approach operates, remind the client about your agreement to review your work together. At the fifth session, for example, consider saying something like this:

> You may remember that we agreed to review what's happened in counselling at the sixth session, which is next week; I'd like to suggest that you think over what you consider you've achieved here and perhaps make a note of any questions, doubts or new goals you may have, and bring them to our next session. How do you feel about doing that?

We have realized, when supervising the work of trainees, that some clients misunderstand the intention of a review session. Certain clients believe that the review will be a kind of assessment of *them*, and this misunderstanding often creates a sense of foreboding for clients. In some cases clients drop out of counselling because they believe they are about to be 'reviewed', or critically assessed, in something comparable to a work performance interview. Some clients specifically interpret a review as an occasion on which you, the counsellor, may decide to tell them that they just cannot be helped, or that you cannot get on with them. It is worth anticipating this possible interpretation so that you can avoid such misunderstanding. Think about what you want from a review session and rehearse, if necessary, the way in which you will describe it:

> I'd like to review our work together at the sixth session. This is something that many counsellors do. It can be helpful because it enables us both to look at what has happened, at what seems to work well and what might be done differently. A review session is not in any sense a judgement on you – I hope that's clear.

It is a good idea to ask the client to formulate his or her own idea of the possible uses of a review session, for example by using analogies. You might find it useful when eliciting views on review sessions, to refer to the client's career planning, for example. Ask her what methods she uses to assess where she's heading in her career; does she ever sit down and reflect on what she's achieved and consider if she can do better, or change direction? Does she discuss her career with a friend or partner? Does she, from time to time, review her CV, make changes to it, and decide on a need for further training? You might use examples other than this, but the point is that by referring to examples from the client's life, you can show that the process of reviewing events in a structured way, where time is devoted to the review, is not necessarily a mysterious or threatening one.

Having prepared the ground for your review, do not make the mistake of ignoring the occasion, or of minimizing its importance. 'We agreed to review our work together today', is an honest way of introducing the session. By asking the kind of question which is commonly used at the beginning of sessions generally – 'How are you today?' – and then allowing the client to continue exploring an ongoing concern, for example, you are discounting the importance of the review. You may think that it is always vital that the clients are given 'space' in which to air any feelings before engaging more systematically in the work of a session. Although there is some truth in this, we believe that this 'space' often displaces all other agendas. If you have clearly negotiated to hold a review session, the client will have mentally registered it, and will be prepared for it. So, clearly raise the subject of review and invite your client to bring in his or her reflections.

Another way in which you and your client may not get the most out of a review session is that it can be cut short by avoidant or vacuous declarations by your client that all is well. 'Well, I can't think of any problems, I think everything is going fine, thanks', may be the reply to your opening enquiry. While acknowledging the client's claim that some sort of progress is being made, be prepared to probe such statements gently. 'It's good to hear that things are going well; can you tell me what, in particular, is going well for you?' is a statement which honours the client's words, yet calls for fuller information in an interested tone. Gently but persistently push for concrete and specific examples of what is going very well, quite well and not so well. Link what the client says in the review with what the original goals in counselling were declared to be. 'I'm glad to hear that you're feeling less depressed because that's something you particularly wanted to change, wasn't it?' is such a linking statement. But do not stop at that level of information-gathering. Ask the client how he or she accounts for the change (see Section 21). What has the client done differently to bring about the change? What have you, the counsellor, done or said that has contributed towards the change? Enquiries like the latter are not intended to solicit flattery or to be reassuring for the counsellor. Their purpose is to identify what has helped the client and what may help even further.

The more negative aspects of a review are likely to be more difficult. The client may think that he or she has not significantly changed, that any change has been for the worse, or that you have not met his or her expectations. The client may be assertive or even hostile enough to voice such negativity, but more often he or she will give non-commital statements, perhaps. When the client says, 'I don't know, really, I suppose the counselling's been all right', you would do well to probe this with, for example:

You say it's been 'all right', but I'm not sure what that means, and I notice that you look rather down in the face when you say it. It's quite possible that you may not have felt good about the counselling, since for many people change takes time. It's also possible that I'm missing something important, so I'm keen to hear from you any doubts you may have.

Convey to the client the message that you have his or her welfare at heart, that you are a professional who is concerned with the quality of your service, and that you place great weight on the importance of factors which are unique to each client. Underline the idea that a central purpose of a review is to identify as precisely as possible any particularly helpful counselling interventions as well as any areas of difficulty for the client, any blind spots you may have, and so on. Convey this with warm interest and not in an interrogative manner. Note the client's mood and style of responding. It is possible that despite your explanations of what a review means to you, it may still have another, more problematic meaning for the client. It may, for example, encourage the client to feel under pressure or 'on trial'. If your client shows such signs, you may attempt to provide reassurance that this is not your intention, or you may decide to ease off altogether. Alternatively, you may sensitively enquire into the reasons for your client responding in such a way.

When a review session works well, the client and counsellor collaboratively summarize their previous sessions and map the progress that has been made towards goals. They are able to acknowledge positive movement and to trace the components that led to it. They can specify which moments within sessions, which counsellor statements, which interpretations, homework assignments and confrontations, for example, were effective or accurate, and which were less helpful. They can both acknowledge their moments of distraction, avoidance or error. They can voice their feelings about each other and how these are either facilitative or otherwise. When high levels of rapport are evident, a review session may be experienced as extremely rewarding.

Many review sessions will perhaps yield modest learning, and may not last an entire session. Your client may be quite willing to mention one or two issues about which he or she feels positively and negatively, you may note these and adapt your approach accordingly, and the session may return to the ongoing work in which you were engaged before the review session. We mention this rather unspectacular scenario because we are aware that some supervisees harbour the fantasy that review sessions should be confrontative, catalytic occasions leading to exciting new insights and behaviour. Obviously they are frequently not like this at all, so do not anticipate achieving too much! On the other hand, consider that a review session is a special and time-allocated opportunity for you and the client to gather thoughts, to summarize issues covered so far, to look closely at the strengths and weaknesses of the counselling relationship and to arrive at a new agenda. By structuring your work in this way, you demonstrate concern to hear the client's feedback. You also introduce the opportunity to alter your pacing. If the client makes it apparent that he or she has not made the level of progress that you had thought, for example, or indicates that he or she is in fact miles ahead of where you thought, you may consider adjusting your pace. Counselling can get into a rut, just as any other relationship can, and a review session, when it is honest, comprehensive, collaborative and purposeful, has the potential to expose and correct such relationship problems. This is especially significant in longer-term counselling, and we advocate regular reviews, every few months (or in some cases, weeks), when you are working with clients over an extended period.

Key point

Think carefully about building review sessions into your counselling work, explain their purpose and note clients' different reactions to them. Modify your practice in the light of the feedback you are given in a review.

Understanding and Working with Effective Tasks and Goals

7 Monitor and improve the goal-directedness of your counselling

By 'goal-directedness' we mean that it is important for you to work with a sense of direction. This is not the same as directing the client against his or her will or against his or her own 'organismic valuing process', and neither are we advocating that you become locked into 'aim-attachment' – that is, feeling obsessively compelled to set, monitor and successfully meet goals with all clients. Implicit in clients coming for counselling is some discontentment with their current situation and a wish, however, vague, for some sort of change, internal or external. Egan (1990) distinguishes between intent, which is a broad awareness of wanting a change; aims, which identify the areas in which the person wishes to see change; and goals, which are committed and specific statements of the kinds of changes the person wants to make. Egan suggests that we help clients through such a sequence, but he also urges counsellors to be 'goal-guided rather than goal-governed'. There is a balance to be found between the completely open-ended, non-directive (and all too often aimless) approaches to counselling, and those which may too quickly and exclusively fasten on specific, discrete goals and their achievement.

The term 'goal' is not of paramount importance. What is crucial is that you and your client have or build a mutual sense of therapeutic purpose. Your client or you may refer to 'objectives', 'preferred scenarios', 'visions' or other expressions of goal-directedness. Often goals are implicit in phrases like 'If only I could be rid of this feeling' (meaning 'I want to feel happier') or 'Why do I always get so confused about this?' (meaning 'I want to understand this better'). If you are in doubt about the importance and usefulness of goals, consider that even in the most distressing of client problems (such as sexual abuse, bereavement, or cancer) there are implicit or explicit goals. But it is important to be sensitive here. You do not say to someone who is crying agonizingly about a sexual trauma, 'So what's your goal?' But at an opportune moment, you would do well to clarify how such a client feels about the past, about him or herself now, about the ability to cope, and by doing so you help to establish healthy short-term and longer-term goals. Simonton et al. (1988) for example, commend the sensitive use of explicit goals for cancer patients.

Sutton (1989) advocates explicit goalsetting. Her argument is that in the bewildering world of multiple therapies, there is no way of evaluating the effectiveness of counselling other than agreeing with clients on measurable objectives. Meaningful goals should have a positive direction (rather than indicate the absence of a negative state) and should be stated in the client's own language and may include, for example, 'That I want to feel more relaxed' (rather than 'I don't want to feel anxious'), 'That I want to be able to complete my college assignments' (rather than 'I want to stop procrastinating') or 'That I would feel remorseful rather than plagued by guilt'. Sutton uses simple progress charts on which clients record their sense of progress towards (or possibly away from) these stated goals, from week to week. Practitioners of cognitive-analytic therapy (Ryle, 1990) also adopt such evaluative procedures. Consider the merits of such devices well before dismissing them; their great advantage is that they do reduce the nebulousness of much counselling.

We realize that many clients are very confused or distressed when initially presenting for counselling, and cannot always state what goals they may have. Consider such a client:

Client: I don't know why I've come, really. I just don't seem to be getting on with things.

Counsellor: You're unsure about your reasons for being here but it might have something to do with a sense you have that you're not getting to grips with . . . with what exactly?

Client: I don't know. With everything really. I mean, I've been meaning to finish my dissertation for weeks, but . . . I just can't.

Counsellor: There may be other things, but your dissertation is one example of what you're not getting on with, and the way you talk about it, it sounds as if you feel quite overwhelmed by it.

This client may well be very depressed generally and the sensitive counsellor will not overlook this possibility, but since the dissertation has been mentioned as a problem (and therefore may indicate a specific goal) it is timely to follow this up:

Counsellor: I wonder if you would think it worthwhile to consider, with regard to your dissertation, *if* you want to complete it, *when* you may need to have it completed by, and any consequences of *not* completing it; perhaps you have some idea too of what's *preventing* you from doing the work. Can you comment on that?

Client: Ah . . . well, I want to finish it, yes, and I'd be in quite a mess if I didn't, but . . . but, yes, I do feel that something's holding me back.

The completion of the dissertation is indeed a goal of the client, but there is now a sense of another kind of goal – the goal of understanding this reluctance. Counsellor and client might proceed to discuss the problem in this direction until clearer goals are formulated. Note two points here. The first is that the counsellor does not force the client into declaring goals when the client is obviously not ready to do so; at this point a sense of direction is enough. The second is that the counsellor is not content to reflect the client's sense of impotence and is not afraid to use direct questions. One of Egan's main criticisms of the helping professions is that too many counsellors remain with clients in the initial, exploratory phase and fail to help them move forward. A certain amount of probing may often be essential before goals can be formulated.

Here are some further ideas on eliciting and clarifying goals. Goals should preferably be specific, achievable, within the control of the person and consistent with his or her value system. Ask the client if there is anyone else who wants the goal to be achieved, and whether the indifference of significant others would have an effect. Is a stated goal the client's or others'? Ask clients to list reasons for the importance of their goals. What advantages and disadvantages attach to achieving the goals? What are the obstacles to goal-attainment? How will it feel to achieve a goal? What subgoals are involved in getting to a stated goal? How can other people and environmental resources assist in attaining the goal? How can goals be maintained? Encourage clients to brainstorm possible goals, especially when they are stuck.

We have had the experience as counsellors of meeting clients who are perfectly clear about their goals, and who wish, for example, simply to be rid of their panic attacks. It can be tempting to try and lure such clients into the 'meta-goals' of exploring and understanding what led to their attacks, even though such conditions are often remedied in a short time without reference to the client's past. Remember that ethically it is the client's right to determine the goals and the limits of his or her interest in counselling. Also note that goals change over time. A client may be content to achieve one goal now, while another emerges later, or the client may even terminate counselling on reaching one goal, and decide to return later with another. Do not have goals for your clients that they do not have for themselves (it is often the case that counsellors have more ambitious therapeutic agendas than their clients). Finally, ensure that clients' goals are therapeutic. A glaring example of a self-defeating goal is an anorexic client wishing to lose weight. Discuss all such issues with clients as early and explicitly as possible, and do not allow an unhelpful divergence to arise between the goals that you and your client believe to be pertinent.

Key point

Attend to goals, whether expressed as such or not, and ensure that both you and the client are committed to working towards them.

---

8   **Vary your use of structuring**

We have explained what we consider the usefulness of and indeed the ethical necessity for structure in counselling from the very beginning (see Section 1). Explicit information given to the client and negotiations made with the client clarify the conditions under which counselling takes place and also invites the client to be an active, equal participant in the entire process. Day and Sparacio (1989: 16) distinguish between structure ('joint understanding between counsellor and client regarding the characteristics, conditions, procedures and parameters of counselling') and structuring ('the means by which the counsellor and client together define the guidelines that govern the counselling process, possibly involving such activities as informing, proposing, suggesting, recommending, negotiating, stipulating, contracting and compromising').

Certain models of counselling and psychotherapy and some practitioners incline towards invariable structure (or 'frame management') and justify this on the grounds that it is therapeutic for clients to know exactly where they stand. According to Smith 'the management of the frame has a more powerful impact upon the patient, for good or ill, than any other feature of the psychoanalytic interaction (including the content of the analyst's interventions)' (1991: 164). This belief stems from the concept of maternal 'holding' and from the claim that all clients unconsciously value and need a 'secure frame' and are threatened by a 'deviant frame'. We do not share this view. Contrary to the 'communicative approach', we have no clinical evidence that all or even any clients are threatened or offended by the counsellor suggesting or inviting requests for some variation of the structure of the counselling process. We consider groundrules important but not sacred.

In Section 5 we discussed the reasons for and uses of varying the therapeutic bond according to client characteristics and preferences. In the same way, we think it is important to be flexible about structuring. This does not mean that you will agree to lower fees, for example, if the client requests this (although you may under certain circumstances agree to this if, for example, the client is suddenly made redundant) or that you or the client will alter agreements in a cavalier fashion. It means that a balance between 'tight', invariable structure and 'loose', accommodating or 'fuzzy' structure is advocated according to various factors. We recognize the client's 'search for structure' (Casement, 1985) and even 'structure-hunger' (Berne, 1970) but we believe structures in counselling both evolve and change healthily by adult agreement.

It is widely recognized that clients who are highly disorganized or fragmented, either chronically or temporarily, need firm boundaries. If you are working with a client who is an acknowledged alcoholic, for example, you will not bend your rules about not seeing your client if he or she arrives drunk. If your client begins to uncover traumatic memories of having been sexually abused in childhood, this is not the time to decide suddenly to take a holiday or to agree to visit the client at home. Consistency of meeting time and place and other basic parameters is generally preferable and certainly so in the examples given here. But consistency with a purpose differs from rigidity.

The other side of the coin may be illustrated by clients who are realistically unable to commit themselves, for example, to regular appointments for financial or health reasons. If you are approached by someone suffering from myalgic encephalomylitis (ME) who wishes to have counselling, but honestly declares that it is not always possible to predict the ability to keep an agreed appointment, or may not be able to endure hour-long sessions, you are faced with deciding between not accepting this person as a client at all, or allowing for a considerable degree of flexibility (see the comments of an ME sufferer, in Dryden, 1992a). If your theoretical approach (or your interpretation of it) dictates that such clients can make regular appointments if they 'really want to', then you will obviously not take on a client who protests otherwise. A more common example in our experience is the client who cannot afford our stated fee, or cannot afford weekly sessions. Like most counsellors we try to offer some flexibility regarding fees and are certainly willing to offer fortnightly sessions to those who request them.

In line with our views on collaborative working, we commend negotiation as to structure. How might a need arise for altering the structure and how would you observe the need, and how would you deal with the subject? First, let us consider a straightforward case:

Client: I was wondering if there's any way we could change our appointment time? Until now it's been OK, but my boss is getting funny about me taking the time off in the day.

Counsellor: Yes, I see. That's fine by me if we can schedule another time convenient for both of us. How about 7 p.m. on the same day? Would that give you time to get here after work?

This is a clear negotiation. It does not assume any hidden meaning in the client's communication, nor does it have the 'feel' of a test of the counsellor's firmness or flexibility. Potentially, there could be an issue of assertiveness involved: has the client buckled to pressure from the boss unnecessarily, or wisely? The counsellor is aware of such salient considerations, is capable of raising them now or later, but decides not to here. Here is a more problematic example:

Client: I don't think an hour is long enough for me. It feels too constrictive. Is there some way I can have longer?

Counsellor: Well, I normally work to an hour but we can consider a longer session if necessary. Can you say something about how the time seems too short?

Client: I'm often just getting to something (I need time to unwind at the beginning and to sink into the feeling that's uppermost for me) and then it feels like . . . like time's up . . . 'too late'.

Counsellor: There's often a feeling for you of . . . it sounds almost like being cheated and like not having your own needs recognized. Is that it?

Client: That's it, yes. So I'd like longer if possible. If it is possible, of course I'm quite happy to pay the extra.

What is problematic about this is that the client's request for extra time may symbolically represent another undisclosed feeling. If you prematurely agree to such a request you may fail to help the client discover the underlying need (for example, to feel special, to be acknowledged, to challenge her mother's rigidity). On the other hand, if you reflexively deny or interpret such a request, you snub the reasonable adult question within it. Why shouldn't the client have an extra half-hour if it is felt to be a need and you both agree on the terms? It is easy to 'stick to the rules' invariably and also to bend the rules to please the client, but it is another matter to engage in mature, responsive negotiation. Guard against becoming *overly* consumerist, by using your clinical experience and hunches about the client. If your feelings about the client are clear, you will have a sense of whether such requests are reasonable or are an invitation to enter into some kind of struggle or into an unhelpful collusion.

The occasion may also arise for you to suggest such changes in structure to your client, for example:

> I've noticed how often you seem to be in the middle of something just at the end of the session; do you think there's some meaning in that for you, or would it be an idea to think about trying a longer session sometime?

If you have been schooled to believe that sessions lasting 50 or 60 minutes are sacrosanct, consider those practices which 'deviate' from this while offering a responsible rationale. Lacanian psychoanalysts have been known to terminate sessions after a relatively brief time on the grounds that the essential work of the session may have been achieved within that time. Behaviour therapists may conduct 30 or 45 minute sessions on the one hand, when specific pieces of behaviour change are addressed, or they sometimes conduct much longer sessions, when, for example, they are accompanying a client on an agreed behavioural assignment outdoors. Primal therapists and experiential psychotherapists, who aim to help their clients into profound, often regressive feelings during sessions, recognize that such work often takes longer than an hour and therefore tend to negotiate sessions lasting one-and-a-half or two hours. The key issues in all such cases are that structuring is negotiated according to a therapeutic rationale and the client's understanding of the rationale and its implications.

Key point

Consider the advantages and disadvantages of varieties of structure for each of your clients, being mindful of tensions between practical, ethical and psychological factors.

9   Focus on one problematic theme at a time

A focus may be considered to be purposeful attention to any client problem or issue within which an underlying theme can be detected. A client may report having a problem with his boss, who is a woman, for example, and it may become apparent that he has difficulties in generally accepting the authority of women. In the early stages of counselling it is often necessary for the client to go into some narrative detail before being satisfied about identifying specific problems. Various themes may then become apparent as problems are discussed. Another client may report, for example, that she feels in crisis about her career; but she has had such crises before and responded by changing career direction. She realizes that she does not want to go on like this, partly because it reminds her painfully of her father's similar tendency to be indecisive; she gives examples from her childhood of how his career uncertainties affected her. So here we have both present-day and historical themes. The kind of focus we are concerned with here might involve, for example, attention to the theme of confusion or apparent helplessness: the client feels, or believes, that she cannot make the right decisions. The career problem in this case may be a manifestation of certain irrational beliefs, such as, 'I must not do the wrong thing' or 'It'll be awful if I mess this up'.

Your arrival at an agreed, manageable number of foci, and indeed at one focal priority at a time, will depend on several factors. There may be constraints on the number of sessions that can be offered, or the client may wish to attend only a certain number, or be able to afford only a certain number. The client may be concerned with one well-defined problem or be overwhelmed by a seeming torrent of problems. You may be influenced by a particular theoretical conceptualization of the client's concerns. We consider it good practice to help the client to prioritize concerns, and offer an explicit rationale for working on each concern in a particular way. Explain your thinking to the client and negotiate (if necessary provisional) agreement to work towards resolving a problem according to your conceptualization of it. Seek the client's permission to interrupt if he or she inadvertently wanders too far from the agreed focus. There is every reason to think that clients will appreciate such purposeful reminders rather than resenting them.

A procedure used in cognitive therapy (see Blackburn and Davidson, 1990) is the listing of problems following initial exploration. This takes the form of a summary at the end of sessions in concrete terms. Its rationale is the reduction of global problems to manageable, and therefore hope-engendering, proportions. Especially when working with clients who are depressed, the counsellor's empathic formulation of precise problems and gradualistic approaches to solving them, offers the possibility of important first steps in coping. Many clients, depressed or not, appreciate the counsellor's efforts to demystify and structure each session in a helpful way. Consider, then, agreeing on an agenda for every session. Use a question such as 'What would you like to devote most of today's session to?' Always remember to check, from week to week, whether the focus and problem you were working on is still relevant and potent, or not. Change the focus on each of the client's problems and their dynamics when you and the client are satisfied that a sufficient degree of helpful new understanding has been arrived at.

It is perhaps a persistent misconception that focused problem-solving is associated mainly with cognitive-behavioural as opposed to 'depth' approaches, and counselling is sometimes pejoratively dismissed as (only) problem-solving rather than radical therapeutic transformation. Hobson (1985), who regards psychotherapy as personal problem-solving, shows that such problem-solving is always mediated by the subtleties of the therapeutic relationship. Hobson's account of 'the first five minutes' of a therapeutic session reveals a tentative yet skilful search for focus and an evolving invitation to the client to disclose his or her concerns about the unfamiliar therapeutic situation and what has brought the client to it. So, eliciting foci and agreement to work in a reasonably systematic way on one focus at a time, need not be regarded as a cold, behavioural exercise. The search for specificity should not, however, become an interrogation, although it does entail questions.

It is not only the client who may be tempted to jump from one subject to another, either defensively or purposelessly. Counsellors too can wander, sometimes because they become fascinated by an essentially peripheral line of enquiry, or they may impulsively seize an opportunity to induce catharsis, or they are defensively motivated to steer the client away from an area which is painful to themselves. Clients who are more compliant may well be seduced away from what is focal for them. This is another good reason for explicit agreements: they also serve to bring you, the counsellor, back to what is pertinent. Naturally, the client's thoughts, as well as your own, will wander both in an effort to understand and in occasional inconsequential associations, but the framework of agreement between you helps to realign the therapeutic conversation.

As with goals, it is important that you do not become obsessive about any particular focus. Heron (1990) warns practitioners against 'the compulsive search for order' and suggests that it is sometimes necessary and therapeutic for clients to 'switch' from one kind of focus to another. Monitor the progress of work on foci and be alert to signs from the client that there may indeed be other significant foci requiring attention. You may, for example, help a client to understand and to change his attitude to his boss, who is a woman, and his attitude to women generally may also change. He may, as a consequence of such changes, begin to want to focus on his sense of identity in a wider way; or he may simply wish to extend his learning 'that I don't have to feel comfortable about my boss' to other 'uncomfortable' situations. Sometimes there will be an orderly sequence of foci, but more often there will be a non-linear movement from one focus to another. Allow for this and check with the client your intuition as to when the time is right for a change of focus.

Key point

Focus on the themes or dynamics which may underlie each of the client's problems and avoid moving from one focus to another without being reasonably sure that the client has understood the dynamics involved.

---

10 Vary your work from a narrow focus with some clients to a comprehensive approach with others

Lazarus (1987) discusses a major turning point in his professional development, when he realized that in certain, but by no means all cases, clients achieve their stated goals yet still complain of areas of dissatisfaction with life. This challenged his allegiance to behaviour therapy and eventually led to the creation of multimodal therapy, which he claims to be 'comprehensive and systematic'. Lazarus is critical of models of counselling which address only one or two client modalities of human functioning when, in his view, human beings in their complexity require systematic assessment of their problems and appropriate interventions to meet each problem area. Nevertheless, he concedes that some clients do not opt for comprehensive treatment, being satisfied with the resolution of one or two distressing problems.

Now, you may not share Lazarus's views, but you are very likely to encounter clients who are content to terminate counselling when their 'symptoms' disappear, or clients who gradually disclose deeper layers of problematic concerns, as well as those who wish to be 'in therapy' for some time in order to examine every possible area of their functioning. In each case, there are different decisions to be made. Some counsellors believe that all presenting problems mask and indicate deeper problems, and others subscribe to a 'holistic imperative' which leads them to feel frustrated by clients who opt for 'symptomatic relief'. Consider your own position on what is, in effect, an ethical issue. Will you try to persuade clients, subtly or overtly, that they need further, deeper and more comprehensive counselling, or will you readily accept their judgement on the matter?

A client suffering from panic attacks, for example, learns that in his case these 'attacks' are associated with a placatory tendency to oblige everyone, taking on every job asked of him. By learning simple assertiveness techniques, he markedly reduces the work he takes on and the resentment and stress that goes with it, and his panic attacks virtually disappear. His counsellor, with whom he has rapidly built a good working alliance, is pleased, but then saddened that the client decides to terminate counselling. The counsellor had begun to note interesting themes in the client's history and had begun to anticipate a rewarding therapeutic journey into the client's interior world. The client, however, had only entered counselling to conquer his panic. This is an actual illustration of a narrow focus remaining such and, in our opinion, legitimately so.

It can also happen, however, as in the case discussed by Lazarus, that a client achieves her initial goals (for example, overcoming agoraphobia) only to feel confronted by an aching emptiness in her life. It is well recognized, of course, that apparently unresolvable problems often enable people to avoid adult responsibilities. Do not automatically assume that once a client's initial goals are achieved, nothing remains to be done. Some clients may be able to tell you that in spite of their progress in counselling they are aware of other concerns that they wish to address. A quite different consideration presents itself, however, when clients are unable to articulate their sense of dissatisfaction. Such clients may well not be eager to terminate, yet may require encouragement and help with formulating further goals. Perhaps their symptoms have served as their way into more comprehensive counselling, or it may be that since they have inadvertently stirred things up within themselves by having counselling, they now feel there is 'no going back'.

Awareness of countertransference reactions in ourselves should ideally free us from having any personal expectations of our clients, yet there are various factors that can militate against our moving freely between the comprehensive and the narrow. The most mundane of these is often our need to earn a livelihood. It is extremely difficult to earn a reliable income in private practice if all or most of your clients wish to focus on narrowly defined, short-term goals. There is inevitably a temptation in the minds of private practitioners to want to 'keep' clients, which can subtly lead to a tendency towards initiating ever-deeper or more wide-ranging work with them. Assuming, however, that you are in a position which allows you freely to work with both short-term and long-term clients, another possible obstacle to flexibility may be the narrowness of your training. If the core theoretical model in which you have trained places emphasis either on specific problem-definition and symptom-removal, or on depth analysis and working through, for example, then you may not be equipped to respond beyond such training. If you suffer from 'therapeutic perfectionism' (that is, wanting to address every conceivable angle of clients' concerns) or anxious attachment to a pure theoretical model, then your ability to move from a narrow to a comprehensive approach with different clients will be limited. We believe, however, that a majority of counsellors are probably at least somewhat eclectic and naturally responsive to their clients' idiosyncratic needs (see Section 28).

Be sensitive to each client and to the intensity, duration and comprehensiveness of counselling from which the client may best benefit. Do not foist deep regressive therapy on someone who clearly only wants to be a little more assertive. Do not brandish a battery of psychological tests under the nose of a client who needs a few sessions of healing grieving. Equally, do not ignore signs or requests for more, different, deeper, broader therapy when it is clear or probable that (in Lazarus's words) 'more is better'. Get yourself into a mind-set and an economic position in which you can creatively and ethically offer what is optimal for the client, and not necessarily what is more comfortable or gratifying for you.

Key Point

Distinguish between clients who prefer to work on specific issues and those who wish to work on broader issues, and offer the most helpful approach accordingly.

---

11 Be flexible using within-session and between-session foci

Models of counselling and psychotherapy differ in the emphasis they place on what transpires within sessions and within the client's everyday life. At the extremes, some counsellors view as enormously, if not exclusively, significant, the relationship between client and counsellor within sessions. Others direct almost all their attention to specific changes in the client's life. The respective rationales are first, that the healing relationship is the fount of all further, solidly-rooted change, and second, that counselling and personal change is principally about grappling with problems and confronting difficulties in the 'real world'. Many counsellors clearly lean in one direction or the other, yet many believe themselves to be concerned equally with within-session and between-session foci. Consider to what extent you are actually flexible in this respect.

One way of ascertaining which kind of emphasis is most likely to make sense to each client is to use a questionnaire of the kind devised by Chris Barker et al. (reproduced in Dryden and Feltham, 1992b). By using the information gained from such questionnaires you can obtain a good picture of whether a within-session focus is indicated, a between-session focus is called for or whether some mix between the two is the best emphasis. Lazare and Eisenthal (1989) identified 14 different (articulated or inferred) 'patient requests' or needs, which ranged from ventilation and psycho-dynamic insight (within-session foci) to advice as to what to do and needed referrals to suitable medical or community facilities. These latter requests and needs might fit either between-session foci (such as, advice on homework assignments) or a focus on a choice of treatment or a referral that is entirely beyond the scope of counselling (for example, residential treatment). What we think is important is not to assume that what clients need matches what we prefer to offer. It is also important not to assume that clients need *either* predominantly within-session foci *or* between-session foci, since each client may benefit from changes of emphasis during the course of counselling.

Let us first examine the error of assuming that all clients need an intensive within-session focus, which has been called 'hot-housing'. A client who sees you once a week (one hour out of 168 in the client's week) may indeed have interpersonal difficulties which could be changed by intensive attention to the relationship with you in the session. The client may or may not, however, respond to such an approach, or the client may overly concentrate his or her energy on counselling sessions and feel better just after them but not enduringly. Some clients, for shorter or longer periods, undoubtedly do need and benefit from intensive within-session work. But if you fail to consider what the client 'does with' the counselling after the session and during the week, and if you fail to note the possible adverse circumstances in which the client may live, you are not offering a balanced perspective. Most clients need a certain level of active participation in their counselling in the sense of internalizing new learning, trying out new behaviour and reporting on the results of such learning in subsequent sessions. If counselling becomes the 'high point' of the week and the counsellor, instead of the client's agenda, becomes the focus, then progress will be impeded and client dependence on the counselling or on you as a counsellor may be fostered.

The opposite error may be made in the assumption, for example, that all clients are mainly or exclusively in need of active counselling interventions which direct them to confront their self-sabotaging behaviour in the real world and not to look at the here and now relationship with their counsellor. This might be referred to as 'cold-housing'! There may be a temptation, when using certain active-directive models of counselling, to seize zealously on particular between-session tasks. In your enthusiasm, you may direct an agoraphobic client, for example, to visit several public places each day for a week. The client may in fact execute this task and it may prove more or less effective. But it is quite possible that the 'fear of public places' was only the tip of an iceberg, or only one of several problems; for example, the client may have suppressed a memory of being raped. If you remain dogmatically and exclusively wedded to your between-session focus with such a client (especially since it appeared to achieve such good results) you may fail to investigate more subtle emotional cues that might be apparent within sessions.

It is unfortunately easy for any counsellor to get into a certain mind-set from which it is difficult to escape. You may go through a phase, for example, following a rather confrontative supervision session, of thinking that you are too warm with clients and you may resolve to correct this by being more confrontative and by refusing to collude with clients' wishes for escapist cosiness in their sessions with you. You may find yourself setting tough new home-work assignments for such clients. When applied indiscriminately, such a concentration on between-session work is unlikely to be helpful. Conversely, if you become aware in supervision of a tendency to be overly concerned with clients' performances in their everyday lives, you may subsequently resolve to focus all your attention on the client–counsellor relationship. These are examples of being unhelpfully over-corrective in your counselling.

Consider the balance of within- and between-session foci applied to each of your clients. Ask yourself what factors may be at work in each case. Is client A persistently avoiding mentioning how he feels about me? Why do I feel that although client B often undertakes and achieves good results with his assignments, something is missing in his understanding?

How might various issues be raised and negotiated? For example:

Counsellor: We seem to spend a good deal of time discussing your relationship with your boyfriend and that may be quite necessary and useful. I'm wondering whether it would help, in addition, if we looked at ways in which you could talk to him directly about some of these matters?

This client has become comfortable discussing her problems in counselling sessions and has begun to avoid taking any action to alter them in her life. Another example:

Counsellor: You've confronted many of the issues you told me were bothering you at work. I wonder how you're feeling about the way things go here, for instance about our relationship?

This client readily talks about his everyday life and actively takes steps to change things, but the counsellor has a sense of 'things left unsaid' within sessions (see Section 19). A more complex example:

Counsellor: I appreciate that it's been difficult for you to try out those 'new ways of behaving' we talked about. I notice too that you sometimes seem to have difficulty raising certain subjects with me. Would it be more helpful to you to practise changing things in here or out there?

This client retreats from both within-session and between-session challenges and the counsellor wishes to establish an agenda based on the client's choice.

In these examples, each client is made aware that their attention has been on certain foci, perhaps somewhat to the detriment of others. The counsellor attempts to draw attention to the significant choices to be made between within-session and between-session foci. If you have not explained such choices to your clients at the contracting stage, raise them for discussion when you later become aware of any such imbalances and explain that it can be useful to concentrate on foci in a variety of settings. A formal review session is a particularly good time to raise and explore this issue (see Section 6). Consult Sections 19 and 20 with regard to within-session foci, and Sections 22 and 24 with regard to between-session foci.

Key point

Be aware of the possible uses and abuses of within-session and between-session foci and alter the balance of attention to each according to each client's prevailing needs.

12   Ensure that you and your client mutually understand and use change-enhancing tasks

Tasks are the means used to approach and achieve the client's goals. Put differently, tasks are the strategies, exercises, disciplines or purposeful experiences undertaken in the interests of the client's goals. Both the client and counsellor have tasks in counselling and the clearer the mutual understanding of these, the better. Every client has to do something (and doing here includes identifying and discussing feelings and thoughts) in order to explore, re-frame and change aspects of his or her life. Every counsellor has to do something to assist this process. Usually there is at least a series of tasks, and these can be analysed into a further set of micro-tasks.

Depending on his or her theoretical orientation, each counsellor will tend to use particular kinds of tasks. You may place great emphasis on contracting, setting boundaries and providing a climate for free association and transference, for example. Or you may view your tasks as primarily the conveying of core conditions. Alternatively, you may employ behavioural assessment, goalsetting and systematic desensitization. We have already advocated that at the stage of pre-counselling information and contracting, you explain your counselling approach in general. As you begin work with each client, you would do well to offer short explanations of your understanding of the client's problems and of what you see your role as being in relation to addressing them. For example:

> Well, it sounds as if you need to talk quite a lot about your parents' deaths and I think it's best for now if I mostly listen and try to understand. Would you agree?

Or

> You keep mentioning the difficulty you have in showing your feelings and I'd like to help you with that, perhaps by pointing out to you when you dismiss or minimize feelings and by encouraging you instead to express them. Would that be helpful to you?

Such statements make your reasoning transparent and help the client to understand your tasks. Too many counsellors, in our view, formulate private hypotheses, often based on theoretical persuasions which are never shared with clients, and test these out with interpretations and other interventions which can mystify and even sometimes distress clients.

Clients, too, have their tasks. These may be quite apparent to them (for example, 'I know I've got to start opening up and talking about my feelings'); they may emerge during the course of counselling (for example, 'It's become clear to me that I want to understand and change the games I play'); they may be suggested by the counsellor (for example, 'I think it might be helpful if you took some time to observe and note down the troubled thoughts you get before you go to work'); or they may be negotiated by client and counsellor together as in the following example:

Counsellor: You're struggling with the decision about your job and I think it might help if you set down on paper the advantages and disadvantages of leaving it. Do you think that might be helpful?

Client: Yes. But I seem to get so confused. I'm not sure if I've got problems because of my job, or if there are deeper problems that I blame on my job.

Counsellor: Right. So would it help to try first to spell out both the real problem with your job *as well as* your other problems, in order to clarify the differences for you?

This dialogue shows the possible danger of seizing on a certain task, and the advantage of fully discussing its appeal to the client. You may still come back to the task originally suggested, but first you need to explore other underlying factors. So be explicit and flexible in discussing and negotiating tasks.

To be most helpful, tasks should take into account the client's personality, gender, race, worldview, learning style, speed and grasp of psychological concepts (in so far as these relate to therapeutic tasks), as well as having sufficient potency to facilitate goal-attainment. There are many references to clients who have been completely mystified by therapists asking them, for example, to imagine themselves as animals or objects, or who have been offered interpretations of their situations which seemed bizarre. Many consumers of family therapy interviewed by Howe (1989) reported that 'they did not know what the family therapists were hoping to achieve, and understood even less about the methods used'. One woman, referring to having been asked to construct a genogram, said, 'I thought, "I don't see the point, but we'll go along with it"; you have to accept the method they use at the clinic.' Sutherland (1992) mentions many examples of unexplained and seemingly wildly inappropriate tasks encountered by himself in individual therapy and by both himself and his wife in couple therapy.

Tasks include within- and between-session work, from the dream interpretation of psychodynamic counselling to the shame-attacking exercises of rational emotive behaviour therapy. A full account of how clients perceive their tasks and of how tasks, including homework assignments, are negotiated, is given in Dryden and Feltham (1992b). As well as the substance of each task, it is important to consider whether clients are in fact able to carry them out, whether they have sufficient resources and ego-strength to carry them out, and whether the tasks themselves are potent enough to meet the clients' needs. All such issues can be clarified by negotiation and subsequent reflection. Guard against the temptation that many counsellors fall into to try out on clients innovative techniques you have just learned at a weekend workshop, for example. Before using any particular techniques, explain them to clients and seek their collaboration, or accept their right to decline.

Another very significant task for the counsellor is to familiarize him - or herself with research (see Section 27) and clinical wisdom regarding interventions of choice. This refers to the concept that certain client problems and conditions are likely to respond well to particular counselling interventions and not to others. Not all counsellors subscribe to such a concept, but we advocate that you consider it carefully in your clients' interests. If, for example, you are presented with clients whose concerns are primarily related to eating disorders, sexual problems, addictions, phobias or compulsions, will you simply offer your preferred orientation without modification, or will you search for and apply interventions found by many of your colleagues to be more helpful for certain problems? You have the tasks of learning what the interventions of choice are, how to use them, how to explain their significance to clients and perhaps, in some cases, referring clients to other practitioners who can offer such interventions. Goldberg (1977) cites a colleague's concern about how often in therapy the treatment is not determined by the patient's ailment but by the therapist's predilection.

Key point

Remember that you have tasks, including the overriding task of addressing the client's 'ailment' and that the client's tasks and your own need is to be as clear and mutually aligned as possible. Ensure that both the tasks you use and those you suggest to your clients have sufficient potency to enable them to achieve their goals.

13   Tailor the use of therapeutic interventions to the client's unique set of characteristics, interests, learning style and other salient variables

We suggest that it is useful to consider each client's personality and culture very carefully. Think about the client's personal interests, hobbies, learning and communication style, cultural and social background, tastes and values. Both you and the client have your own unique characteristics, some inherited and some chosen, which have the potential to enhance or diminish the therapeutic relationship. As Ivey et al. put it, 'there may be four participants in the interview: the counselor/therapist and her or his cultural/ historical background and the client and his or her cultural/ historical background' (1987: 94). A word of caution is necessary here in order to challenge the idea of simplistic cultural or ideological matching. Although it is often advantageous, for example, for a woman counsellor explicitly to bring her experience as a woman to her work with women clients, it is not invariably the case that all women clients will share particular 'feminist' views with the counsellor (see Walker, 1990, for some of the arguments on this issue). It is also true that when issues of race, class and sexual orientation are evident, it may not be helpful to assume that each client feels disadvantaged, oppressed or marginalized. So, while we commend the practice of carefully considering each client's culture, gender, and so on, we also advise against you making unwarranted assumptions about how important each of these factors is to your client.

Omer (1990) suggests that joining at the level of the patient's experience is a key means of enhancing therapeutic impact. The client's life experience is not only one of pain, psychopathology and problems in living, but also one of everyday, family, recreational and occupational pleasures and interests. It is important to note that such experience is not only mediated through words. Omer notes, for example, that certain clients relate more effectively to practical tasks than to talking therapy. Because of the individual's background and predominant learning style, it may sometimes be helpful to identify methods of change other than those dependent on speech. This could entail accompanying the client somewhere, helping with the accomplishment of a practical task, or encouraging the use of creative media (such as painting and drawing) in counselling. Some clients find the entire concept of sitting alone in a room with a stranger and struggling to find words to convey their circumstances and problems extremely unfamiliar, daunting and in some cases impossible.

Remember that not everyone is readily able to talk intimately and in psychological terms. Many people need at least an initial bridge of ordinary conversation about everyday tangible interests before 'opening up'. Howe (1989) found in his interviews with predominantly working-class consumers of family therapy, for example, that they would have developed more rapport had they been offered a cup of tea, some informal 'chit-chat' and other familiar tokens of reassurance. Howe's distinction between 'problem anxiety' (which propels clients to seek help) and 'service anxiety' (that is, clients' anxiety about having an appointment in a strange setting with unfamiliar professionals, and apprehensiveness as to how they may perceive and treat them) is a useful one. Since most counselling and therapy is offered by white, middle-class professionals, this may well arouse greater 'service anxiety' for working-class and black clients.

Ivey et al. (1987) distinguish between individual empathy and cultural empathy. This distinction acknowledges that it can require additional effort, if not training, to grasp and respond adequately to the client's cultural history, circumstances and beliefs. The phrase 'listening with the fourth ear' has been used of this further empathic requirement. Where the picture becomes complicated, we believe, is in the individual's own experience and interpretation of his or her culture and the adherence to or struggle against its norms. Add to this the individual's personal tastes, interests, aspirations and the occupational and recreational cultures in which he or she partakes, and you will realize that individual and cultural empathy needs to be exercised in many subtle ways.

Rather than struggling or even pretending to understand cultural and other experiences that are very different from your own, we suggest that you note and, if deemed helpful, honestly disclose such difficulties to your clients, for example:

> I think I understand you, but it would help me if you could tell me a bit more about ... the country where you grew up/the regime under which you lived/the sense of 'daily pressure' you say you feel, living in a new country/your religion/your community.

Some clients may consider that they should not have to explain, and some may benefit from a suitable referral, but many will appreciate your honesty and interest. In certain extreme cases, for example refugees who have been severely traumatized, clients may be terrified of explaining their backgrounds and you should be alert to such possibilities (see van der Veer, 1992).

The point has often been made that emotional repertoires and vocabularies vary widely from one culture to another. Heelas (1985) cites the Chewong people, who are aboriginal Malaysians, as having a very limited emotional vocabulary. Since their culture is unusually non-violent, speculation arises as to whether they *suppress*, or simply experience very little anger or aggression. Similar considerations are crucial to counsellors. What is psycho-pathological denial of emotion, and what is a validly *different* cultural and emotional experience from your own? If you are a white, middle-class and middle-aged male counsellor who is trained and steeped in the methods and values of humanistic therapy, for example, how will you construe the possibly muted expression of a young woman refugee from Malaysia? What stereotype do you hold of 'macho men' or 'hysterical women', for example?

Therapeutic interventions are mainly delivered in words and most counselling has the character of a conversation. From the field of socio-linguistics, Tannen (1992) observes that individuals' conversational styles are learned in families as well as within wider cultures and individuals frequently misunderstand subcultural linguistic nuances. She extends this problem to counsellors, contending that often differences in conversational style lead to 'unwarranted psychological evaluation' of clients' concerns. In other words, skewed communication is by no means always evidence of personal psychopathology. According to Tannen, 'we tend to think in the terms and related concepts our language gives us' and 'people who enter psychotherapy or join a religious or human-potential movement soon begin to talk differently' (1992: 163). The use of therapeutic concepts can be helpful, but it can also slip into jargon and mistaken assumptions. In so far as counselling and psychotherapy constitute a kind of culture – which generate a great deal of specialist language – you may be in danger of thinking and communicating too automatically in unhelpful psychological terms.

One means of correcting this tendency is constantly to refer to the client's 'frame of reference'. How does the client construe, not only his or her problems but also everyday life and expectations? What are the idiosyncrasies of the client's conversational style? How does the client spend his or her time? What is important to *the client* (not to *you*)? Emmy van Deurzen-Smith (1988) addresses such questions from an existentialist perspective. The personal meanings, values and aspirations of each client need to be identified and utilized as part of counselling. Whether clients express an interest in gardening, surfing, tennis, aerobics, poetry, bingo, dreams, computing, music, social work or parenthood, these are subjects containing keys to their values and the way in which you respond, engage in their interests and bother to learn the language of their everyday concerns, is likely to enhance or diminish your therapeutic partnership. Do not confine your interest in the client to the deep, dark, complex and problematic: respect the ordinary, everyday ongoing realities of clients' lives.

We have worked with clients who are practising musicians and sportspeople and have often found it very beneficial to link their ideas of problem-solving within artistic and physical activities, to problem-solving at the more emotional level. Consider, in your own work, making use of explicit analogies between the coun- selling process and learning processes with which your clients may be more familiar. One of us worked with a man whose music was such a central part of his life that no counselling relationship would have been possible without constant references to it, in spite of the counsellor's own musical illiteracy! What counts is not your expertise in the client's interest or activity – although you may fortuitously have such expertise and use it to good advantage – but your willingness to get to know what it means to the client. In some cases, it helps to know the kinds of films, music and literature by which clients are excited or moved. Knowledge of this kind can open possibilities for improved understanding of clients' philosophies or their predominant emotional patterns. Sometimes a depressed client describing a favourite film may show you a glimpse of inner emotional richness that could not otherwise be made known. Elicit such information with genuine interest (false and patronizing enquiries will obviously not help) and if necessary ask clients to describe their intimate, everyday and idiosyncratic world, for example by completing a self-characterization exercise (Fransella and Dalton, 1990).

Each client's unique background will dictate to some extent what his or her anticipations of and preferences for counselling are. In Section 5 we have looked at how to vary your relational stance, according to what clients perceive to be most helpful. Fish (1973) puts forward the view that a central component of therapeutic effectiveness stems from the counsellor fulfilling the client's beliefs about the counsellor's power. Fish advocates that counsellors become aware of and utilize fully the power of belief within the client. By learning what kind and degree of power and status each client invests in you, you are in a position from which you may consciously choose to reinforce the client's beliefs, *in the interests of enhancing therapeutic progress*. When a client from a particular culture perceives you, for example, as a powerful doctor-figure, you may be able to use such culturally-embedded perceptions to enhance the therapeutic bond and to hasten progress. Conversely, when it is apparent that there is a significant mismatch between your client's preference for a helping relationship based on egalitarian principles, then you will need to adapt accordingly.

Key point

Get to know as many facets of your client's unique experiences of life as possible and use this knowledge to inform and improve your counselling relationship and interventions.

14   Adjust your pace to the client's pace, information processing style and other learning variables

In Section 13 we looked at how improvements in counselling may be made by noting, learning from and making adjustments to counselling interventions, in the light of clients' personal interests, learning style, communication patterns and so on. Here we examine the importance of pacing and its implications for counselling. Most of us probably have a working pace that is natural and comfortable to us. Instinctively we adjust to each of our clients according to their personality, the nature of their problem and the stage of change they are at. We learn to discriminate between the depressed person's slowness, the leisurely pace of someone from a family which is very relaxed and the 'passive-aggressive' unwillingness of some clients who stubbornly refuse to reward our therapeutic efforts with responsive movement! It may help you to consider which of your clients is a constitutionally fast learner, who has a 'hurry up' driver, who is anxious to make a 'flight into health' and so on. Ask yourself why your clients differ in the speed at which they learn and move in counselling. Do not overlook individual and group differences in communication patterns. Tannen (1992) comments that 'microseconds of pause' in conversation can mean a great deal. British speakers are found to leave longer pauses than Americans, for example, and a failure to understand such differences may seriously affect the success of counselling.

It is more difficult, however, to identify the features of your own pace. Reflect on how monotonous or variable, how responsive or indifferent to the learning needs of clients, your speed of delivery is. Your approach to counselling is also coloured, of course, by your culture, personality characteristics, pathology, theoretical orientation and other factors. Counsellors are probably drawn to certain models of counselling partly because of the conception of time and change implicit within them. While the person-centred and psychodynamic approaches are not notably hurried, rational emotive behaviour therapy and intensive short-term dynamic psychotherapy, for example, are not notably leisurely. You probably have certain vague expectations of how long counselling should take, on average, and this sense of time colours the pace at which you work from the very beginning. It is a good idea to ask clients at the beginning of counselling, 'Have you thought about how long this might take?' Based on fantasies and fears about counselling, on the urgency of particular problems, on the availability of money and time, as well as on the person's normal rate of (emotional) learning, conceptions of time and pacing will vary considerably. Goldberg has a definite view on this matter:

> The more uncertain and vague the period of treatment and the goals to be worked on, the greater the influence of irrational and magical notions and attitudes the client may have toward therapeutic work. The more specific the period of treatment and the goals to be worked on in treatment, the more appropriate and rapid the confrontation with these refractory attitudes in the work to be accomplished in therapy. (1977: 46)

The way in which you have described counselling and your particular approach to counselling at the contracting stage, will have influenced subsequent pacing. Notice whether you do allude to how long counselling may take or not. If you do, what anticipations are you helping to create with respect to the likely pace of counselling, and if you do not, what is your rationale for not being explicit about time (and what will be the effect of this on the client)? An excellent way of reviewing your attitude to the use of time is to study tape-recordings of your work (see Section 30) and to ask yourself what your predominant pace is, whether and how it varies from client to client, helpfully or not, and how it could be changed. You can learn a great deal about your pacing from audiotapes of your sessions. If you tape-record a whole series of sessions you may be able to detect significant changes in pacing. Clients do not necessarily learn, speak and react at a uniform pace throughout the course of their counselling and therefore you may improve your counselling by considering and adopting variable pacing.

Of paramount importance is the match between your pace and that of your client. If you impulsively rush your client you are likely to lose him or her; the client may attempt to keep up with your pace and may give an outward appearance of compliance, or may alert you by facial signals, for example, of the difficulty he or she is having. If, on the other hand, your client is naturally quick-minded and you tend to be rather slow or ponderous in your manner, then you run the risk of frustrating the client. It is thought by some that it is easier for constitutionally fast-thinking counsellors to slow down for clients than for constitutionally slow-thinking counsellors to speed up for their (fast-thinking) clients. This is something you can monitor in your own practice. Keep in mind the question: is the pace at which we are working conducive to the client's learning regarding the client's natural learning style, and the effect the client's problems may be having on his or her ability to learn? Clients who are experiencing depression or confusion, for example, may require extra consideration and what Casement (1985) refers to as 'unobtrusive availability' rather than questions and challenges.

It is recognized that in cases of post-traumatic stress disorder (PTSD), for example (see Hodgkinson and Stewart, 1991), it is helpful if a counselling response is available quickly following the appearance of stress reactions. If you are ready to meet your client's urgent needs and understand the nature of PTSD, you are challenged to adapt your pacing accordingly. You must judge to what extent you encourage the client to confront painful images or allow the client to avoid them. In such cases you may need to challenge the defensive pace at which your client indicates he or she wishes to work. In this situation, you must question whether you are pushing the client appropriately, but equally you must ask yourself about the wisdom of letting the client avoid what is unpleasant but probably necessary. Similarly, in cases of complicated bereavement generally, you may be in the position of having to challenge the client's defensively chosen pace. These can be very difficult decisions to make and are an example of how you may benefit from consulting relevant research (see Section 27) and from discussing such issues in supervision. When you are unclear whether a client is a naturally slow learner, or that learning is affected by circumstances, consider asking directly: 'Have you noticed recently that it's taking you longer to think and talk than before all this happened?'

Take into account all the above factors as well as those discussed in Section 13. Is your client someone who needs to chew things over, who likes to read up on things and prepare well before taking action? Does your client like to plunge into things? Does he or she process information rapidly or slowly, using imaginative connections or careful cognitive strategies? At what stage of change is your client (see Section 16)? Do you get the sense that there is a mismatch between your preferred pace and the client's and if so, can you adjust accordingly? If you are able to review tape-recordings of your counselling with such questions in mind, you will find that it is possible to learn a great deal and to improve accordingly.

Key point

Do consider the matter of pacing and your attitude to the use of time, and find ways of monitoring how well you adjust your pace to that of the client.

---

15 Use the 'challenging but not overwhelming' principle

The 'challenging but not overwhelming' principle (Dryden, 1991b) is based on the concept of optimal arousal. Clients learn best, it can be argued, when they are exposed to a productive level of emotional arousal. Too much pressure within the session is likely to lead to counterproductive anxiety or demoralization, whereas too little pressure can lead to an atmosphere of stagnation and cosiness. A high level of challenge can under certain circumstances with some clients produce rapid and dramatic results. This is the case in Davanloo's (1990) intensive short-term dynamic psychotherapy, which utilizes 'unremitting pressure' with certain clients in order to test and break down defences. Even Davanloo, however, acknowledges the need to discriminate between those clients who are ready for, and can tolerate such a level of challenge, and those who cannot. Egan (1990) suggests that reluctance to challenge clients is probably a wise 'starting position' but that enduring reluctance to challenge throughout the counselling process is not in the client's best interests. In his view, clients are frequently much more robust than counsellors give them credit for being.

At least two issues are involved here, then. One is the judgement as to optimal levels and kinds of challenges for clients. The other is your willingness and ability to provide those levels. Let us look first at how you might calculate clients' needs for challenge and their abilities to deal with them. Some clients are notably highly aroused when they present for counselling; they may talk rapidly, cry a lot and have difficulty containing themselves and finding a focus. It is more useful in such cases to attempt to reduce a client's level of emotional arousal, to help them into a productive zone of moderate feeling (for example, by helping them to focus on chosen subjects or thought patterns) than it is to reinforce or increase their emotional arousal. Conversely, when clients are moderately depressed it can be very helpful to introduce emotional challenges, for example by identifying and exploring even small signs of sadness or anger. Ware (1983) gives an account in transactional analysis terms of how different personality adaptations can be identified and what may be the best (and worst) ways of productively challenging in each case.

The second important issue concerns your ability to perceive, understand and skilfully act on each client's need for challenge. Consider that counselling is by its very nature somewhat stressful and unfamiliar for the client who is likely to be experiencing many emotions including both the 'problem anxiety' and 'service anxiety' (Howe, 1989) that have been discussed earlier. Consider too that most clients present with a combination of willingness and resistance. They want to change and are wary of change. Your clients have a conscious therapeutic alliance with you, but also, as Davanloo (1990) argues, they may have an unconscious therapeutic alliance with you that in effect is saying, 'I want you to help me in spite of my resistance and I give you permission to challenge me, even if at times I appear uncooperative'. If you are convinced of these factors you will be ready, when you consider the time is right, to overcome any resistance you may have to challenge therapeutically. Equally, you will be sensitive enough to note when you may be too zealous or driven by countertransference, and you will be ready to modify or halt your challenge.

Consider the following example. Jean is a woman in her 30s, a bookkeeper, who lives with a man with whom she often argues. She vaguely feels that things could be different, is unsure how, but doubts whether her partner will change. She thinks she may want to have a baby but her partner does not want any children. She wonders about ending the relationship but is afraid that she will suffer emotionally and may not meet anyone else. In counselling sessions she works very slowly, apparently needing to take things in and to turn them over deeply. When attempting homework assignments (for example, making a list of what she would really like for herself and what she is afraid of) she does not get very far. The counsellor helps her to identify aspects of her poor self-image, sensing that she has got herself stuck in a poor relationship because she thinks it is better than nothing and that probably no one else will have her anyway. The counsellor encourages her to consider and undertake any small acts of assertiveness she can, to observe herself relating to men in general and to note how she judges and withdraws herself. She finds even these tasks difficult. The counsellor uses mild challenges involving her beliefs about him: does she think the counsellor finds her boring, unattractive, and all the things she thinks about herself? She finds this level of challenge difficult, but productive; with some discomfort, she begins to allow herself to experience and to talk about her self-image, and to challenge it herself.

For some clients direct interpersonal challenges within the session (immediacy) produce the most useful level of therapeutic challenge. For others, mutually agreed graded homework assignments are more fruitful. With many clients a combination of such challenges works well, and of course each client may well at different times respond to different levels and kinds of challenges. Think in terms of keeping the heat on an issue, maintaining a degree of healthy challenge within sessions. Balance this against clients' overt or non-verbal protestations or signs of acute discomfort. Introduce clients to the concept of 'challenging but not overwhelming' (Dryden, 1991b: 135), describe the relative benefits and appropriateness of tolerating 'discomfort anxiety' and invite them to tell you what the optimal dose of challenge is at each stage.

Key point

Calculate and deliver the optimal level of challenge that is likely to help each client at different times in the counselling relationship.

III

Identifying and Addressing Clients' Obstacles to Change

16 Be mindful of and guided by the client's stage of change

A helpful model advanced by Prochaska and DiClemente (1984) is known as the 'stages of change' model. This sets out to describe transtheoretically (as a model which can be applied to all clients by counsellors of any orientation) the different stages of change in which clients present for counselling. These are known as the pre-contemplative, contemplative, action and maintenance stages. We will look at each of them and their implications for practice in turn.

Pre-contemplative stage

In this stage a person may have no sense of having a problem at all and no intention of seeing a counsellor. He or she may however present for counselling at the behest of someone else (a spouse or parent, for example) or may be referred involuntarily, by a Court or other statutory agency, for example. The person may pretend to go along with the idea that there is a problem he or she wishes to work on or may defensively deny the problem. Because of this remoteness from any feeling of ownership or responsibility for whatever the problem may be, it is often impossible to work with someone in this position. On the other hand, there may be a glimmer of motivation providing the counsellor with an opportunity to describe what counselling can offer. Sometimes such a person may appear uninterested or unimpressed but may have registered your explanation and your non-threatening concern and decide to come for counselling later, either to you or to another counsellor. Someone in this stage of change may easily elicit bewilderment and frustration in counsellors. When you suspect that a client is in this stage, actively, but in a warm and not overzealous manner, seek information on his or her views of counselling and the views of those who may have urged the client to ask for counselling. Do not expect enthusiasm or cooperation and avoid dismissive or judgemental reactions in yourself. An example:

Client: Well, my manager said it would be a good idea for me to come for counselling. Things aren't ideal for me, but then they're not for anyone, are they? I don't really see how you can help me, to tell the truth. I know I've just got to pull myself together, that's all.

Counsellor: You've told me that you're under a lot of pressure at home and I appreciate that you accept responsibility for dealing with that pressure. In the meantime your work is apparently suffering. I may not be able to help directly, but people often do find it useful just to let someone else (someone not involved) see and hear what strain they're under; and sometimes by sharing these things you can gradually get some new perspective on them.

Client: Yes, well, maybe, I don't know.

Counsellor: I can see you're not sure about this and that's fine. I'll be pleased to tell you any more about counselling you might wish to know, but otherwise we can leave it there and you're free to telephone me at any time if you decide you'd like to talk over things.

Contemplative stage

In the contemplative stage clients are usually aware that there is something wrong in their lives; there is a problem, even if it is hard to define. The person may still be somewhat hesitant, unsure of what is involved in coming for counselling or wary of what he or she may discover about him- or herself. It is likely that the problem or discomfort in the person's life is sufficiently pressing or unavoidable to make 'retreat' a less viable option. Unlike someone who is in the pre-contemplative stage, this person is actively wondering what can be done about his or her concerns and what can be done to help. This person is ready to explore his or her concerns, however tentatively. You will recognize that such clients are not backing away from you and are not claiming to have been sent or to have no real problems. Equally, they may not necessarily be highly motivated, eager to examine themselves and full of insight and commitment. Rather, they are 'ready enough'.

How might you help someone who is at this stage? Consider the example of a client who has been involved in a road traffic accident, following which she has felt the need to have time off work because of 'nerves'. She understands to some extent that it is normal for someone in her circumstances to feel somewhat insecure for a while, and she has been advised to contact you for counselling. She soon begins to realize that her response to the accident is indeed normal, but that talking about it helps her to come to terms with it. As the counsellor, you realize that she is in the early stages of recovery from shock; she is moving towards using help and realizing that eventually she will need to take action to get herself back to work. You may decide to probe tentatively into any tendencies she is exhibiting to avoid discussing what has happened. But you might also decide that she is not ready to plunge herself back into her old working routine while she is still fairly fragile emotionally. Your interventions will be suitably facilitative, perhaps, but not hurried or in any way suggesting that she is malingering.

At this point we must make it clear that clients do not fall neatly into such categories. You are more likely to identify someone as being roughly pre-contemplative or contemplative, or somewhere between. But in addition to this, be alert to the probability that the same client will be at different stages of change in relation to various personal concerns. So a client who is having difficulties at work, for example, but is not prepared to talk about them, may be quite ready to discuss a wish to give up smoking, fear of flying, or whatever. Do not pigeon-hole clients as belonging to one stage or another. This model is an aid to understanding and intervention and is not in any sense a hardened, diagnostic device.

Action stage

Clients presenting in the action stage, or having worked through from the contemplative to the action stage, appear motivated, energetic, cooperative and eager to become engaged in the counselling process. They are ready to do something about their problems. As a caricature, this is the 'dream client', the person who is 'a pleasure to work with'. Some inexperienced or particularly idealistic counsellors declare a preference for working with such clients and may even claim not to take on clients who make any less commitment than this. We consider this an untenable position. In our experience, clients present in a wide variety of states of motivation, understanding and commitment, frequently depending on the nature of their problem. Depressed clients are not likely to resemble clients who seek counselling as an interesting 'personal growth' experience, for example. But some clients are undoubtedly more prepared than others; they may have worked through much of their concern before coming for counselling, or indeed may have had counselling before. A complication of the action stage is that an apparent commitment to active 'work on the self' may conceal avoidance of deeper-level change. Accept the client's report of how they stand in relation to problems, but also note the possibility of subtler, deeper, masked or related problems.

Let us look at an example of a client in the action stage. A man in his late 40s reports that he has been suffering from stress reactions and realizes that he needs to do something about the way he works. He acknowledges that he works too hard, accepts work assignments from his seniors even when he knows he does not have sufficient time to complete them, and hence stays late at the office, becomes exhausted, and gets into arguments with his wife. This man has identified his main problem and rapidly learns in counselling what he needs to do about it. He accepts that he needs to be more assertive about what work he will refuse to do and also that he would benefit from examining his own irrational thinking about what may happen to him if he simply works sufficiently hard rather than working in a way that is endangering his health and his marriage. As the counsellor, you practise 'skilful neglect' of certain peripheral details of his story, you help him to focus on essential priorities and to make a commitment to putting his insights into action without delay. With such a client, there are compelling reasons for being action-oriented; lengthy exploration of the client's early childhood experiences, for example, is unlikely to be helpful in this instance.

Maintenance

Clients who have progressed through previous stages (demonstrating ambivalence about change, being ready to begin to reflect and move, and working commitedly at change) must also face the task of consolidating their gains, of finding ways of internalizing new learning, reinforcing new behaviour and sustaining the ability to feel and think differently. Clients in this stage are likely to be realistic, to know that change does not come, or stay, easily; they realize that hard work is called for. Maintenance entails the practice of new behaviour, the taking of risks to consolidate learning derived from the previous two stages and preparation for possible relapse (see Section 23) as well as the client's appreciation of just how much change has been achieved. This may not be the most dramatic stage of counselling and in some ways it may be an anticlimax, but without negotiating this stage realistically clients may slip back into their 'old ways'. Someone who has learned how capable she is of academic achievement, for example (as in the film *Educating Rita*), needs both to continue to work hard at that achievement and to deal with those factors which may hold her back (such as significant people in her life who do not want her to change). See Sections 21 to 25 for examples of the kinds of interventions that are likely to be of most help to clients in the maintenance stage.

According to Prochaska and DiClemente (1984) it is quite common for clients to move through the stages of change with forward and backward steps, sometimes even moving from pre-contemplative to maintenance stages only to slip back again 'to the beginning'. A good example of this phenomenon is the person who attempts to stop an addiction, for example to smoking, and goes through a process of giving up and staying off for some time before relapsing, and then perhaps giving up again. So as well as looking for the subtlety of clients being at different stages of change with different problems, look for previous change attempts and anticipate normal human backsliding and even complete relapse.

As we have noted, this model may apply to any client and to any theoretical orientation. It recognizes that both positive change and the tendency to relapse and avoid realities are common human experiences. In assessing new clients or in struggling to understand their difficulties, you are likely to be helped by observing that all clients do not start their therapeutic journey from the same place. Adjust your anticipations and interventions accordingly. Use the reflection process to put it to your clients that they appear to be somewhat hesitant, tentatively committed, impressively engaged or realistically prepared for challenge to their new-found resolution. Elicit their views on this. It can even be useful to share this model with them and to explain that everyone has different starting points for each of their major concerns. Discussion of this model can be used pivotally to help you and your client negotiate priorities, pacing and other strategies.

Key point

Sensitize yourself to the stage of change your client is at according to each of the client's major concerns, and offer interventions designed to match his or her particular needs in that stage.

---

17   Discover the client's past attempted solutions to problems and create distance between such strategies and what you will be offering

Rarely does anyone, on encountering a problem in living, immediately pick up the telephone to make an appointment with a counsellor! Common initial problem-solving strategies include: denying or trying to deny that the problem exists; distracting oneself with activity; breaking down under pressure of the problem; blaming others or expecting others to resolve or remove the problem; hiding from the problem with the use of alcohol, for example. These are some of the more passive and negative responses. Some people attempt to analyse and understand the problem alone, or with help from psychological literature or in conjunction with astrology, meditation, positive thinking and other techniques. Some readily consult partners, friends, colleagues, priests and other carers. Some turn to self-help groups, social workers, counsellors, psychotherapists and doctors. We are *not* suggesting that all attempted solutions are failures. They may be partially successful, successful for the time being, or successful enough to make the person wish to gain further or surer under-standing. However, many people will have consulted a counsellor or similar helper before seeing you.

Many counselling theorists from diverse schools agree that human beings from birth onwards attempt to learn the best possible solutions or adaptations in adverse conditions, or simply as part of their normal human development. Unfortunately, we often misidentify solutions, process information incorrectly, enter into a lifelong 'script', transfer feelings inaccurately and unhelpfully from one person to another, and so on. Casement (1985) asserts that the client's 'stages of growth' are re-enacted in therapy, often in the form of a search. The client's 'search for responsiveness' in the counsellor may be met with 'further substitute gratification' or with a new and healing response. We suggest that you explicitly raise and explore the subject of previous attempted solutions. Be mindful of what the client is prepared to tell you and also of what may be withheld or conveyed indirectly. When a client says, 'Yes, I saw another counsellor but he just kept sitting there and saying nothing', it may mean that it was a model of counselling that was not congenial or helpful to the client. It could, however, indicate that the client feels threatened by silence or by the prospect of relating intimately to a male counsellor, for example. While we advocate that you avoid duplicating a failed or unsatisfactory therapeutic experience, we do not suggest that you think and respond in simplistic, 'either–or' terms or become a mere 'substitute gratification' compensating for clients' earlier disappointments.

Suppose that a client has discovered in previous counselling a tendency to intellectualize and you have been sought out as a Gestalt practitioner who, the client hopes, will counteract this intellectualizing. You may then be able to demonstrate confidently that your approach will indeed confront this avoidant intellectualizing. (Again, we are not suggesting a *simplistic* adaptation on your part to the client's views and wishes.) But you may have a new client who tells you, for example, that a previous counsellor 'kept wanting me to say how I felt about *her*, and I hadn't come to talk about her, but about *me* and *my* problems'. This client may have consulted a psychodynamic counsellor who rather heavy-handedly attempted to elicit transference reactions, or who was perceived as doing so. Suppose that you too are a psychodynamic counsellor. How would you respond? We believe that any sensitive counsellor, of whatever orientation, will recognize and respect 'where the client is at'. In this example, such recognition might take the form of an affirming, 'So it was quite unhelpful for you, then?' But a better alternative might be, 'Well, it is helpful for some people to explore their feelings by expressing how they feel about the counsellor, but I think what would be more helpful for you is to talk about how you feel about yourself; would that be better for you?' Such a statement makes it clear that you have heard and respect the client, that you understand the particular need and you are capable of offering an approach significantly different from that which was previously found to be unhelpful. Your concern in such circumstances will be to avoid offering 'more of the same'.

If the client succeeds in unconsciously enmeshing you in his or her 'games' or self-sabotaging strategies and you unwittingly collude, or you are unable to produce sufficiently creative and potent strategies, you run the risk of becoming part of the problem rather than part of the solution. By discovering what has not worked and what is not working for your client, and by explicitly agreeing on new and more helpful tasks (see Section 12), you place the counselling relationship in a position of 'leverage', from which 'actions that can make a difference' begin (see Egan, 1990). Counselling aims to move beyond the intrinsic fascination of intrapsychic exploration to changes of attitude and behaviour. The client's search, as described by Casement, must be matched by the counsellor's search for effectively different strategies and solutions.

De Shazer (1985) bases his approach to (brief family) therapy on the acknowledgement of clients' successful and partially successful solutions to date, as well as an ongoing search for creative solutions. De Shazer's approach shifts the weight from anticipations of client resistance and discussion of failure and pathology to solution-creation and expectations of change based on it. This approach incorporates a 'do something (anything) different' technique, whereby clients in an impasse situation are asked to respond to their chronic and recurring problems by deliberately and experimentally trying anything that is different from their habitual responses. While we do not suggest that you capriciously and injudiciously try out this technique, we do invite you to consider it as an analogy for the problems you encounter as a counsellor working with clients.

Key point

Offer 'something different' from that which has been done with or by your client previously and guard against becoming part of the 'more of the same' syndrome.

---

18 Discover and deal with the client's obstacles to change at each point of the counselling process

Obstacles to change are of course present from before the client enters counselling. Section 16, on stages of change, explains the progression that clients commonly make, from the pre-contemplative (unmotivated) stage, to the active and committed stages. As the counsellor, you can do nothing about pre-counselling obstacles to change but you are well-advised to consider the variety of possible obstacles which may present themselves at any stage of counselling. We have mentioned the 'service anxiety' which is an obstacle for many clients who are uncertain about how they will be received and treated by professionals. More systematically, Pipes et al. (1985) have examined a host of client fears which deter them from beginning counselling or cause them to delay their help-seeking. Such fears include ideas that counsellors will judge them, will find them strange or crazy, will label or not understand them; that they may be required to do things they do not understand or wish to do, and so on. When we become socialized as counsellors we quickly forget, perhaps, just how unfamiliar and alarming it can be to admit to having problems and to confide in a stranger.

Consider the kind of obstacle which a client may encounter in her own life. She is unhappy generally, let us say, but particularly about her marriage. Her partner has no interest in counselling or wish to be involved in any 'soul-searching' or 'navel-gazing'. She has become uncomfortably aware that she married the wrong man or that she has matured faster than he has and she realizes that by coming for counselling she is taking a first step in what may well lead to divorce. She may have a lot tied up in her marriage economically, perhaps, and so stands to lose much if she does go ahead with counselling and gains the courage to put her dis-contentment into action. A similar predicament is experienced by the secure employee who feels stifled at work but stands to lose out professionally if he really gets in touch with how unhappy he is and decides finally to leave his job.

Such issues may be very conscious but none the less threatening. As the counsellor you will need to help the client explore the possible losses and gains involved, without assuming that the 'personal growth imperative' is what the client will opt for. As Tschudi (1977) has so well pointed out, every such dilemma and obstacle involves a personal value system and pay-offs and comforts in not changing. Orientations such as transactional analysis, rational emotive behaviour therapy and cognitive-analytic therapy also identify well the many kinds of irrational ploys and subterfuges that may be involved. At an early stage in counselling, however, it is useful to help the client assess the advantages and disadvantages of change and non-change. This is best done in an atmosphere of respect for the client and with patience.

As well as specific obstacles related to circumstances, clients may have unhelpful ideas about counselling and about the nature of personal change. Some, for example, imagine that counselling can magically transform things by means of the counsellor's expertise and that it will be an effortless venture for them. Some believe or hope that it will not be painful or uncomfortable. Ellis (1985) lists many kinds of resistance, including the 'healthy and normal'; that which is linked with severe disturbance; those emanating from fear of discomfort and shame and hopelessness; those involving rebelliousness; secondary gains and hidden agendas. He also points out that many obstacles stem from the client–counsellor relationship and the counsellor's untimely interventions. Be alert to the possibility of all such obstacles appearing. At the beginning of counselling, however, as part of your reflection process and evolving contract with clients, raise any observations you may have made about the client's resistance. 'I notice that whenever you begin to talk about your husband, you quickly change the subject' or 'I have the feeling that perhaps you're not comfortable talking about these things with a man' are the kinds of straightforward statements you can make to begin exploration of possible obstacles. Do not, however, make the assumption that the client *does* have the obstacle that you perceive him or her as having, or that the client is necessarily conscious of it, or indeed that it is *the client's* obstacle (it may be a form of resistance coming from you). Put such observations tentatively and openly admit that you may be wrong.

Obstacles can arise both within sessions and in homework assignments, or simply in the client's everyday life. A client may find that when trying to speak to old friends in the intimate way that he or she learns to speak to you, for example, the friends react coldly or unhelpfully. Section 21 looks at the nature of the change process and it can help if you explain to clients how universal such obstacles are. Counsellor self-disclosure can be very helpful in such instances too, as long as it is well-timed (for example, 'I know that when I was in my own therapy some years ago, it took some time for me to understand that my friends didn't necessarily like all the changes I made'). As you move into the middle phase of counselling it becomes more and more likely that, having uncovered perhaps the easier or more urgent matters, the client will begin to experience more chronic, painful, complex or disturbing feelings, memories, thoughts and doubts. Such experiences need not become insurmountable obstacles, provided that you are ready to identify them, to discuss them with your client and to decide together on any necessary changes in your way of working. A strategy that has worked well in the beginning may no longer prove so effective, or the vigorous pace at which you have worked, say, may need to slow down considerably. Towards the end of counselling, too, look out for obstacles to ending, for example in the client growing extremely dependent on you.

Throughout the counselling process be mindful of what you may contribute towards obstacles. Do you or the setting in which you work exacerbate client fears? Lazare and Eisenthal (1989) note that many clients in certain settings (such as a psychiatric outpatient clinic) experience difficulty in asking directly for what they want and do not necessarily find it easier to be asked directly. Phrases such as 'Do you know what you hope to get from coming here?' or 'How would things look if someone could help to transform your life?' are sometimes more useful than direct, psychologically-phrased questions (such as 'What symptoms are you experiencing?' or 'What are your goals?'). Guard against being overzealous, expecting rapid improvements in clients, as well as against punishing clients, however subtly, for not apparently appreciating your hard work or warm concern. And finally, realize that for some people certain changes are not always possible or timely. People in certain circumstances cannot actually change their predicament and may well need to learn to accept it.

Key point

Consider, raise for discussion, and adapt to accordingly, the many obstacles to progress that can arise for clients within themselves, in relation to you or to others throughout the counselling process.

---

19 Monitor and learn from things left unsaid

There is good reason to believe that a significant determinant of how well the counselling relationship develops, is the amount and quality of disclosure compared with 'things left unsaid'. Regan and Hill (1992) have researched the frequency, content and valence (the range from very negative to very positive) of things left unsaid about behaviour, thoughts, emotions and clinical conjectures in brief therapy. They found, not surprisingly, that clients are more likely to hide negative than positive feelings about the counsellor and that sessions are often felt to be unsatisfying when things are left unsaid. Regan and Hill note that clients' concealment of thoughts and feelings may be due in large part to a fear of offending the counsellor. They discovered that counsellors' perceptions were least accurate regarding clients' negative reactions in sessions and that counsellors could identify only 17 per cent of things clients reported as having been unsaid in sessions. The authors point out that clients do not necessarily want to disclose more than they have and particularly in brief therapy may decide to withhold certain information or feelings.

In spite of obvious problems with an area of research that is at an early stage, we believe there are important indications for practice here. In a pilot research project that we ourselves conducted with people who had had successful and unsuccessful experiences of counselling, phrases such as 'I just couldn't tell him [the counsellor]' and 'I tried to tell her but she was so enthusiastic that I was afraid to offend her' were very evident. Mearns and Dryden (1990) conclude in a study of the client's experiences of counselling that 'the unspoken relationship' may be a key factor in both successful and unsuccessful counselling. Significant unspoken material, especially when cumulative, can sabotage counselling altogether, for example when clients drop out of counselling feeling that they are not understood. But equally, when what is unspoken can be identified and worked on, it can become a source of new impetus. In the Mearns and Dryden study a client admits, 'I became quite skilled in avoiding areas which were unsafe for me in the interaction between us'. We believe that such avoidance and evasion is likely to be lessened if, from the very beginning of counselling, genuinely open communication is modelled and explicitly encouraged. Where a reflection process (see Section 2) becomes the norm rather than the exception, the client has at least the permission and channel to voice what may be difficult to voice, and the counsellor too can legitimately claim the right to ask for information.

What kinds of things are left unspoken in counselling? Clients may be completely unconscious of certain things about themselves, which the counsellor may or may not sense or guess at. Material which is distant in time (in the client's life) or which is painful, traumatic or embarrassing, may be suppressed consciously or unconsciously. In the here-and-now of the counselling session, the client may avoid commenting on his or her feelings about the counsellor (the client may find the counsellor awkward, unhelpful, unattractive, or especially kind or attractive) or about counselling itself (the client may find it strange, painful, expensive, aimless or threatening). There may be matters which do not appear relevant for discussion (for example, the client may not bring up the subject of sex because the intention in coming for counselling is to overcome specific anxieties about public speaking). It is quite common for clients to talk about what they think about certain problems but to avoid showing how they *feel*. Clients make their own judgements about how deeply they wish (or can afford) to delve into their psyches and therefore may instinctively avoid certain subjects which do not bear on their current, pressing concerns.

Counsellors too leave things unsaid. The research of Regan and Hill (1992) shows that counsellors often suppress their clinical conjectures, for example. This may be a wise strategy in order to avoid pre-emptively categorizing, labelling or frightening clients. Counsellors were also found fairly frequently to avoid stating their emotional reactions. This finding may be related to the status of the counsellors used in the research (they were still in training) or to their brief therapy remit, but it also poses the question as to whether training induces self-consciousness and caution. It may be that honest, spontaneous disclosures by the counsellor as to how he or she feels about the client may sometimes help more than cautious, professional behaviour. Mearns (in Mearns and Dryden, 1990: 133) tells a client 'I have been feeling especially close to you and aware of just how much you shared with me last week', and this disclosure prompts one from the client. Person-centred counsellors may be more inclined to value genuineness and to trust in their ability to know when their disclosures are and are not likely to be well-received, than practitioners from other schools. It seems likely, however, that all counsellors are aware of feelings and thoughts about their clients that they judge to be relevant or not, safe or not, timely or not, and so on. Section 20 of this book looks at such areas of practice.

Do not become hypervigilant with regard to possibilities of things left unsaid and do not keep anxiously asking the client if there is anything he or she needs to say! Rather, over the course of sessions, note what the client does not volunteer or appears to suppress. Sometimes there are obvious omissions in a client's story, for example no mention whatsoever of the client's father, of any feelings, of sex, or of any social life. When it becomes clear that certain areas are consistently omitted or avoided, it can be useful to point this out and to enquire whether the subject seems irrelevant or painful to the client. Do not ask critically or intrusively and indeed do not ask certain things at all if you are receiving clear non-verbal signals that certain subjects are unwelcome. (You might venture to say, 'It seems that the whole area of sex is one that you'd rather not discuss; am I right about that?') If you develop the practice of asking the client for a problem list, as is done in cognitive therapy, you may refer to this list and ask if anything has subsequently arisen which the client would like to add to it. Another useful question can be, 'If a good friend of your's were to hear you discussing your problems here, would she notice anything obvious that you've omitted?'

Key point

Think about and explore the possible meaning and effect of those things which both you and your clients choose not to say in counselling sessions.

20 Attend to and learn from your own feeling reactions to clients and use this learning accordingly

A large element of counselling is comprised of the counsellor's 'use of self'. The counsellor's own history of suffering, personality structure, self-awareness gained through training and personal therapy, combine to act as an intuitive template when working with clients. From the moment you first speak to a new client, for example on the telephone, impressions are formed by each of you. Such impressions are probably correctly known as 'vibes'. You are aware of what the client is saying, with what sense of urgency, with what degree of insight, helplessness or eagerness, in what tone of voice and with what kind of initial response to you. Even at this early stage, you may find the client highly emotional, agitated, depressed, 'gamey', or motivated, for example, in ways that resonate positively or negatively with your own personality traits or current life crises. Clients often remind us of the more (and less) significant others in our own lives, to varying degrees. Possibly more problematically, clients may also strike chords in us in those areas where we have developmental lacunae, and we can find ourselves particularly attracted to such clients (for example, a client may be struggling to express the more creative, daring, sensuous side of herself and we are aware that these areas are also underdeveloped in us).

This subject is, of course, generally referred to as 'counter-transference'. We unavoidably have feelings about each of our clients and psychoanalysts now generally accept that counter-transference often contains important and useful clues to helping clients. An essential lesson for counsellors is to accept the reality that they have such feelings, which may be very powerful, may be felt as physical sensations or images, may often be ambiguous, but can often be harnessed for gaining understanding of clients. Crowley (1988) distinguishes between (evoked, irrational) counter-transference, and 'appropriate, unexaggerated, non-defensive and non-anxious reactions'. You may, for example, have conscious and rational protective feelings towards a young female client who does not realize how vulnerable she is. But equally, you may have strong protective feelings towards certain clients who are not apparently vulnerable. In such cases, you may unconsciously be confusing the client with someone else (or yourself), you may be intuitively in touch with the client's disguised vulnerability, or you may unconsciously be responding to the client's unconscious invitation to rescue her from adult responsibility. By noting such a feeling, rather than dismissing it as an intrusion from your own stream of consciousness, you can subtly monitor its persistence, precisely what seems to trigger it, and whether it ties up with the client's stated problem or problems. In due course, if it is likely to be helpful, you may choose to disclose this feeling and engage in exploration of its origins. It is the persistence of such feelings which often indicates their significance.

As Winnicott (1949) has shown, it is possible for therapists to experience extremes of feeling towards clients and for those feelings to be primarily about the client and both unavoidable and useful in working with them. It is easy to believe that certain clients are 'just boring' or that we are not on their wavelength, when in fact the 'boredom' we are feeling is a powerful message from and about the client: the client may be projecting hopelessness or protecting him- or herself from painful intimacy by preventing you and others from getting interested, for example. A lesson to be learned here, then, is not to assume that your first interpretation of your feeling reaction (for example, 'He's just so despicable, I can't work with him') is correct or comprehensive.

Wachtel (1985) uses the concept of 'cyclical psychodynamics' to refer to the ways in which clients repeat dysfunctional patterns from childhood in many situations, in a 'circle of causes and effects'. As the counsellor, you can easily become part of this circle of self-fulfilling prophecies unless you are sensitive to the kinds of feelings evoked in you. Wachtel argues that counsellors can effectively help to break such patterns behaviourally by refusing to reinforce them. While transference and its interpretation may sometimes be helpful, another tactic is for the counsellor to think in terms of extinguishing dysfunctional behaviour by consciously and consistently not rewarding it.

Robertiello and Schoenewolf (1987) offer in amusing and instructive vignette form, examples of therapist errors involving countertransference and counter-resistance. These include erotic, sado-masochistic and narcissistic countertransference, and cultural and characterological counter-resistance (such as ethnic bias, fixed social values, chronic depressive tendencies). Their account shows not only how obvious such errors can be, but how commonly they are made. Our comment on this is that it is better unashamedly to note, accept and begin to work on such errors than to deny their existence. As we have argued, by accepting and using your feeling reactions, you can also advance your understanding of clients.

Maroda (1991) suggests that counsellor neutrality and inter-pretation have serious limits and that attention to countertrans-ference and appropriate countertransference disclosures adds much to the therapeutic process. She further points out that the coun-sellor can often help clients by being able to accompany them imaginally into their feelings. When counsellors have explored and resolved aspects of their own lives which have been problematic, they are likely to be able to help clients with similar concerns; conversely, there may be problematic limits to counsellor empathy when the counsellor has avoided exploring certain areas of him- or herself. The more experiential or affective therapies (for example, see Mahrer, 1989) rely heavily on the ability of counsellors to enter the stream of the clients' feelings through their own affective memories, openness and congruence, but all counsellors benefit from being able to tune in finely to feelings and to separate their own from the client's dynamics.

For all the above reasons, we believe that the personal develop-ment of the counsellor, for example through personal therapy, can be a valuable aid to professional development. Unfortunately many counsellors-in-training appear to keep their personal therapy discrete from their work with clients. There is a temptation, perhaps, to take selective material to supervision, to use personal therapy for broad or pressing personal issues, and to give insufficient attention to the emotional impact that clients have on you. Reference to the parallel process in supervision (where the counsellor's behaviour unconsciously re-enacts aspects of the client's behaviour) can be useful, but may not be capable, particularly in group supervision, of exploring the counsellor's feelings in sufficient depth. Counsellors are sometimes told in supervision that 'This sounds like an issue you would do well to take to your own therapy.' How often such issues do find their way into counsellors' own therapy, to take precedence over other issues, we are unsure. Consider, then, the usefulness of examining your feeling reactions to clients in some depth when you are involved in personal exploration, for example in your personal therapy.

Key point

Sensitize yourself to the range of feelings different clients can evoke in you and reflect on what meanings these may have and how they may be used therapeutically.

IV

Helping Clients
to Consolidate
their Change
and Move On

21 Understand and capitalize on client change; attribute change to clients and empower them

Your client begins her session with, 'I've had a really good week. I told Steve that I didn't want to see him and he accepted that, and in general I've found it much easier to talk openly to people.' What do you say? To reply with 'That's really good' followed by silence or inadequate acknowledgement of the change reported by the client, is to miss a valuable opportunity. Since change is such a central factor in counselling, it is important that you encourage exploration of how change comes about. Both you and the client can benefit from investigating how and why changes have been made or not made. What attitudes and actions of the client have contributed to things being different in her life? Has her different attitude affected others in her life and elicited new and preferred responses from them? If so, how has this happened? Without sensitively probing beneath factual statements of change you may not discover the dynamics involved.

In the above example, you might ask 'In what way did you tell Steve that you didn't want to see him?' or 'Can you give me some examples of other interactions you've had with people this week that you've found easier?' You might follow these up with questions such as 'What was it that enabled you to tell Steve this week, when you've been avoiding it up until now?' and 'To what do you attribute your ability to talk more openly to people?' More generally, you might ask 'What have you learned from talking to people in these new ways?' Encourage the client to analyse her successes and in addition to imagine possible contributing factors in her success. She can then be encouraged in future to imagine further possibilities for change. Remind her of the difficulties before she discovered that she could do these new things and ask her if she recognizes the changes fully. It is quite in order to react with pleasure to reports of change, but we suggest that it is usually more effective in the long run to praise the client's effort and commitment than to praise the client as a person.

When investigating the nuances of such changes and the client's understanding of them, it is important to discover whether, or to what extent, the client perceives herself as the agent of change. Does she think that she was lucky; that things just fortuitously went her way this week? Does she believe that you, the counsellor, have masterminded the changes for her or that simply 'being in counselling' is somehow responsible? These are crucial distinctions to make, and to make early on in the counselling process if possible, since counselling is an aid to more effective living and should be a process of empowering clients from the beginning. Point out to the client the new attitude and behaviour that *she* has committed *herself* to and followed through. Remind her that *she* is working on *her* goals and that you are a catalyst in the process, perhaps, but certainly not a puppeteer who is doing her work for her! In cases where clients do tend to attribute great and magical powers to you, monitor any tendency you may have to feel flattered and omnipotent and reinforce instead the client's own motivation and responsibility. (We are not suggesting that you discount the sometimes potent part you play in the client's change process, but that you put it in perspective and realize that counselling is not primarily for your gratification but for the client's growth.)

Consider the phenomenon of 'flight into health'. This occurs when clients report early, often dramatic improvements in their situations. Sometimes such reports are accompanied by a declaration that no further counselling is necessary. Now, there may be genuine cases of such rapid change; sometimes clients are indeed helped by a single meeting with an understanding listener, particularly if the timing of such a meeting is right. Indeed, single-session therapy by design (see Talmon, 1990) relies heavily on such factors. But apparent dramatic improvements can also mask underlying resistance to deeper counselling and avoidance of more painful material. A client may genuinely *feel* better after talking cathartically about problems and feeling heard and understood, but may not necessarily *get* better. Psychoanalysis recognizes that insight and catharsis can feel subjectively like a solution to one's problems but that there may still be much work to do. Rational emotive behaviour therapy stresses the need for hard work on personal change. If you detect that your client has a somewhat simplistic and unrealistic view of change, probe a little in order to discover how deep or real the reported changes are. Are they simply circumstantial and insubstantial changes? Avoid discouraging the client, but encourage the client to question how robust these changes are.

Of course, some clients, unlike the woman in the example given above, will report 'Well, I don't feel any better. I did the things we talked about, or some of them, but I'm still feeling the same.' Some clients may report no change in spite of effort and others may have made no particular effort. The counsellor can apply the same investigative principle to reported non-change as to change. What has not changed? What anticipations and hopes of change did the client have? How has the client acted this week in ways that have reinforced stasis rather than change? What attitudes and behaviours underly the client's inability or difficulty in carrying out any change efforts? Such questions should be put helpfully and with sensitive timing. Confrontation is helpful when the client can accept and make use of it, but depressed clients, for example, will usually have great difficulty initially in entertaining new thoughts or behaviour. Help your clients to develop an attitude of 'personal science' or an enquiring attitude towards their own behaviour and the dynamics of change. Discover whether clients harbour unrealistic beliefs about the nature of change (for example, that it should be easy, dramatic or linear) and explain that the change process varies from person to person. It usually involves both forward and backward steps. It is rarely magical, more often requiring dogged determination and hard work than dramatic, life-transforming insights.

De Shazer (1985) offers some provocative insights into the processes of change. He notes that it is often a very powerful intervention to congratulate clients on how well they have coped with past or present situations and that they are well placed to tackle their new challenges. He also alerts counsellors to cases where 'only a small change is needed'. Some clients magnify their problems, or aspects of them, and can be helped to put them in a new and more realistic perspective. Mastery of small changes may be enough to tilt the balance for some clients away from demoralization to gradual hopefulness. This is a key skill in empowering clients: instead of agreeing how overwhelming their problems are, consider eliciting their existing strengths and acknowledging the changes, however small, that they have already made. Talmon (1990) who, like de Shazer, is concerned with the question of how clients can be empowered in a short time, suggests that the message 'I believe in you and your ability' is not just words. Counsellors need to be highly aware of the danger of clients embarking on a 'flight into dependency' on counselling. While helping clients to explore and understand the process of change, a fine line may be observed between the genuine empowerment of clients, genuine concern that they should not deceive themselves about the realities of change, and the dangers of dependency on counselling.

Key point

Discourage clients from discounting changes they have made and help them to identify the factors involved in such changes. Encourage an attitude of positive enquiry, but take every opportunity to help clients to attribute their gains in counselling to their own efforts.

---

22 Encourage clients to generalize their learning

In this Section, as in Section 10, we wish to distinguish between the smaller and larger goals of counselling. Here, we are concerned with how each client may be helped towards the larger goal of general problem-solving and hence a more satisfying life. Specific successes in counselling may tempt you and your client to remain at a particular level of learning. This can get you trapped in what Heron (1990) calls 'ground floor only' interventions, which ignore possibilities for making connections between one problem (and its resolution) and another, and which fail to identify problematic themes which recur for clients. Counsellors have an opportunity to offer psychological education to their clients that goes beyond concrete and discrete problem-solving. Exactly how you do this depends in part on your orientation (psychoanalysts, of course, tend to dwell on connections between the client–counsellor relationship and the client's historical relationships). What we wish to advocate here is that you look for opportunities, when appropriate, of helping your clients to generalize from one specific situation to other similar situations, with the aim of increasing their repertoire of coping skills.

You may *assume* that what your clients learn in the consulting room, they will necessarily generalize to other situations and relationships. We think this assumption is untenable, since it is quite possible, and observably the case, that for some clients counselling becomes an end in itself and does not produce results in the 'real world'. Where intensive transference or other psychologically compelling phenomena occur within counselling, we suggest that you question their goal-directedness and invite your client actively to make links between such experiences and everyday life. In primal, redecision and experiential psychotherapies, for example, the client is encouraged to experience deep emotional states, but subsequently is also strongly encouraged to make cognitive, imaginal and behavioural connections and plans based on such within-session experiences. 'Can you imagine how you're going to deal with your boss next time you see her?', or 'Now that you've felt how that childhood decision was made, what do you think you're going to do when a similar situation comes up, perhaps tomorrow with your wife?', or 'So you weren't allowed to be angry and expressive then, but now you can be', are examples.

Depending on your main theoretical orientation, you may concentrate primarily on the client's past, on the here-and-now relationship between the client and yourself, on the client's prevailing thought patterns, on key problematic situations in the client's everyday life, or on long-range strategies. We have already discussed the idea of negotiating your approach with clients. Whichever way you have begun to work, when the time comes for broadening out from the specific to the general, you need to rediscover the client's views on the approach you are using. Does your client see how the events of childhood relate potently to making changes in his or her present fear of flying, for example? When the client is ready to confront further problem situations in his or her life, spend some time eliciting whether the client understands the applications of your approach to new problems.

If your client agrees that certain early goals have been successfully accomplished and would like to tackle others, consider drawing up a hierarchy of difficulties. Let us say that a female client, who has begun to feel more confident in her interpersonal relations, confesses that her ultimate fear is of making public speeches. She realizes that she completely avoids such a fear by ensuring that she never undertakes any work which would require it, yet at the same time she experiences a nagging sensation of wishing she did not have to hide from such situations. Now, to jump from modest, small-scale interpersonal improvements to large-scale public speaking engagements is probably not realistic. But you may ask the client for a list of situations involving speaking to different groups of people, and ask her to rank them in order of their anxiety-inducing associations. The list may read:

1 Speaking up occasionally at an evening class.
2 Giving a short presentation to a class.
3 Speaking up occasionally at a sales conference.
4 Giving a formal presentation to a group of strangers at a seminar.
5 Giving a formal presentation at a large conference.
6 Taking part in a theatrical presentation.

Even without acting on such a list, the items raise potentially useful information for therapeutic work. What do these situations have in common? What precisely does the client fear about them? What is she predicting will happen to her, for good or ill, in each situation? Does she really want to achieve such feats? What does she stand to gain by aiming for or avoiding these situations? If she were to undertake to tackle such situations, what time-frame would she give herself? In a case such as this, the items given may not be very realistic, but none the less give you and the client a direction to work towards. Using the 'challenging but not overwhelming' principle (see Section 15), you can encourage the client to select useful targets and to suggest the pace at which she needs to work. This process of negotiation is itself growth-enhancing and part of 'learning about learning'.

One means of providing a bridge between the consulting room and the outside world is role-play. You can serve as the client's feared 'other' to whom she wishes to speak, while she is filled with anxiety. Alternatively, imaginal exercises can be very powerful. Sometimes it is best to conduct these with closed eyes ('You are standing on the platform, there is a sea of faces before you, the microphone close by . . . what are you feeling?'). Connections between the outside world and the counselling room may also be 'reversed' to advantage. When a client, for example, protests that men are so awful, they never listen, they have no feelings, you, as a male counsellor (in this case) may ask her to direct such statements at you in order to experience the impact and explore it further. Be alert for opportunities to help clients to generalize their learning beyond particular problem situations; equally, respect clients' rights not to so generalize.

Key point

Help clients to see the usefulness of applying what they learn
in counselling as widely as possible in their everyday lives, if
they wish to do so.

---

23 Anticipate and address relapse

Closely related to our discussion on encouraging clients to
generalize their learning is the issue of relapse. Progress in
counselling is rarely, if ever, entirely linear and successful; rather, it
may follow contours of flatness, large or small breakthroughs,
digression, regression, disillusionment, hope and dogged working-
through. But even when the overall pattern of counselling is clearly
successful, the counselling must one day end. Even when a client
has made powerful or dramatic changes, possibilities for relapse lie
ahead. We believe that any model of counselling which fosters a
once-and-for-all hope or promise of secure and unassailable
improvement or cure is mistaken. Just as it is magical thinking to
enter counselling hoping for a counsellor to banish all ills, so it is a
form of magical thinking to suppose that a certain period in
counselling, however long, provides a seal of immunity against
future disappointments, temptations and even utter relapse! Please
note that we are not advocating a message of doom and
despondency, but one of realism.

If you accept the wisdom of introducing the subject of possible
relapse, then it follows that strategies for relapse prevention are
called for. The first step in any such strategy is to identify a
productive moment at which to bring up the subject with your
client (presupposing that the client has not raised it). Although you
may begin work with a client who has already made previous
significant gains and wishes you to help with maintaining those
gains (see Section 16), with a majority of clients you will probably
be starting counselling 'from scratch', and only gradually coming to
the point at which substantial gains have been made. Generally, it
is fitting that early sessions in any counselling relationship

engender hope and facilitate working through issues as constructively as possible, but once a number of significant gains have been made you have the opportunity to broach the subject of relapse. To some extent such discussion falls naturally between celebration of successes and anticipation of the end of counselling. To some extent, too, such a discussion comes more naturally into counselling where the client has had concerns relating to serious self-defeating behaviour (for example, problem drinking, drug abuse or damaging personal relationships). But all client problems contain possibilities for relapse. For example:

Client: I think I've really come to grips with my relationship. Tina and I are getting on much better now.

Counsellor: Yes, I'm pleased at how things have improved for you. You tell me that you rarely fight now and that you usually are much more ready to talk and to do your bit around the house. We've talked about how the changes have come about and it seems that largely it's because of the effort you've made, and you've been able to offload some of your angrier feelings here. I suppose what I'm wondering is what you'll do when things perhaps don't go so well at home, or when you feel you don't want to make the same effort.

Client: It doesn't feel that way at the moment. I think I've covered a lot of ground here, I've understood a lot more about myself. I suppose . . . well, if I have an off-day I'll have to remind myself of what we talked about here.

Counsellor: Right. Like most people, you're quite likely to have at *least* one off-day once in a while! You say you'll remind yourself of our discussions. Can you envisage just how you'd do that, when you would fit it into your 'off-day', and how you would make it an effective reminder?'

Client: I . . . I'd need to acknowledge to myself when I'm obviously about to get into that state of mind. I'd need to sort of stand back. But . . . I'm not sure what you mean.

Counsellor: I think you're picking up the idea, but I'll explain. We tend to believe sometimes that everything is now fine and we don't want to be reminded of the past. That's understandable. But if we're going to be honest and realistic, it's good practice to consider how we will handle old patterns if they do reappear. That's what I'm inviting you to do, and I don't mean it to sound at all demoralizing.

In this example the subject of relapse has to be raised without any lead-up to it, which demands a special sensitivity from the counsellor. Other clients may well ask you, 'What shall I do if I lose my nerve?', or they may indicate a lack of confidence about coping without you behind them. In all cases the rationale is similar: not to deal with the possibilities of relapse leaves the client vulnerable. However, responsible postponement of discussion of the subject of relapse, at sensitive times, for example, or with particularly fragile clients, is another matter: do use clinical judgement. In the example above the client begins to identify his own strategies for coping with relapse, which might be developed much further by using, for example, mental rehearsal in which he is encouraged to imagine a scene where everything is going wrong again, how he feels about it, how he construes it, and how he may constructively handle the situation. Lazarus (1981) uses the colourful phrases 'anti-future shock imagery' and 'emotional fire drill' to refer to such relapse prevention strategies and their rationales.

Consider clients' unique vulnerability factors as well as the kind of predominant problems they have been dealing with in counselling. Use whatever means are helpful to identify with the client what environmental challenges, for example, may prove especially difficult. Are there particular places, friends, temptations, situations in which the client is likely to have these new-found strengths sorely tested? If necessary, encourage the client to brainstorm possible relapse situations. The client may be feeling completely in control now, but what if he or she were to find him- or herself lonely, weak and without support, for example? Do not introduce such imaginary scenarios in a way that will foster demoralization, but rather as a creative, well-timed challenge. If the time is right with a particular client, consider using 'worst scenario' challenges in order to encourage mental rehearsal.

You may need to judge finely the times and the degrees of challenge you choose to talk about relapse. In cases where someone has conquered a particularly stubborn and dangerous habit (drug addiction, for example) it may be inadvisable to encourage too much thinking about the habit. For some clients it works very well to have them confront actual problematic situations to test themselves out, but for others this may not be appropriate. If you can, encourage a good deal of relapse prevention work towards the end of counselling. It is also an effective strategy to schedule a follow-up session some three or six months later, or sooner if necessary. This often has a psychologically containing function, the client being enabled to separate from you and to rely on his or her own resources, while knowing that you are still there.

> **Key point**
>
> Do not avoid the subject of possible relapse; rather, encourage the client to consider it realistically and to prepare strategies for meeting and overcoming relapse.

24   Encourage clients to be their own counsellors

It has been pointed out, for example, by Norcross (in Dryden, 1991c), that clients usually try to make some of their own changes before counselling and often with at least partial success. Counselling need not be seen as something done instead of, or as something that is superior to, self-change. Indeed, Rusk (1991) advocates 'guided self-change' as a method of personal growth which pays more than lip-service to the idea of empowerment. As counsellors we are trained to use concepts such as enabling and empowering but we may sometimes forget just how important they are. Rusk suggests that we move towards becoming egalitarian consultants to our clients in their own self-actualization. There may be a relatively short period of intensive counselling (or a longer period for those clients in acute crisis or who are severely disturbed) but most clients, he argues, are capable of active, guided self-change without too much dependence on their counsellor.

The first step in encouraging clients to be their own counsellors is to examine how you really feel about this issue. The greater your tendency to regard clients as deeply damaged, riddled with unconscious conflict and in need of extensive psychological expertise, the less likely are you to trust the concept of guided self-change. But if you have observed the undoubted strength and integrity that most clients do have, in whatever degree, and especially if you have witnessed clients making changes in their lives in a relatively short time, you may realize that a little counselling can go a long way and that clients need only as much counselling as is necessary to become their own counsellors. Let us make it clear that we are not devaluing counselling, or underestimating the greater need that some clients have for a safe, partially dependent therapeutic relationship. What we are saying is that the goal for all clients is autonomy and personal growth (although clients may not use such terms) and this does entail learning that the counsellor is primarily an aid in their moving towards that.

Rusk endorses the use of clear contracts, variations in structuring counselling (including meeting outside the consulting room), between-session homework assignments and tape-recording of sessions. Interestingly, Rusk views such tape-recording as being not for the benefit of the counsellor's professional development (see Section 30) but for the client to learn from. In addition to the taping of sessions, consider an exercise sometimes used in personal construct therapy, called 'McFall's Mystical Monitor' (see Burr and Butt, 1992). The client (in this case, a woman) is instructed to speak on tape for an hour or more, in the privacy of her own home, about a pressing problem; if she 'dries up' she must explain into the tape-recorder why she has done so, and keep talking. She rewinds the tape, listens to it and erases it. She then repeats the exercise, this time for 30 minutes, then listens to and erases the tape. The point of this exercise is that the client becomes her own counsellor, realizing that the problem always was and always will be her's to solve.

Homework assignments prepare clients to become their own counsellors (see Dryden and Feltham, 1992b, for various examples). We recommend 'bibliotherapy' as an extremely useful way of helping clients to think about change processes. There are many excellent self-help books on the market and, although you need to exercise some discrimination in which of these you suggest to your clients, it is well worth suggesting a few which are pertinent to your client's problem. Such books are also often written to be compatible with particular theoretical orientations. One such is *Feeling Good* (Burns, 1981) which introduces clients to the theory and application of cognitive therapy. Bibliotherapy may not be recommended for clients who have difficulty reading or who are compulsive intellectualizers, perhaps, but otherwise it has the advantages of encouraging the client's active participation and of accelerating the counselling process. If you believe all self-help books make extravagant claims, read Burns's chapter 'Dare to be average: ways to overcome perfectionism'!

Clients often report that they have imaginary conversations with their counsellors during the week, or during longer breaks, as well as after counselling has ended. In a sense these conversations are discussions clients are having with themselves; they have internalized the therapeutic alliance and are now setting their own agendas. While such memories of the counsellor and extensions of such memories into imaginary discussions on new problem situations are helpful and benign, the eventual goal is for the person to become his or her own counsellor. You can assist this process by encouraging clients, within sessions, to be their own devil's advocate, to begin the process of self-disputing and self-coaching. For some clients the process of keeping a counselling diary proves to be particularly effective. Help the client to discover the most effective ways available to suit his or her learning style, whether it be reading, writing, tape-recording, artwork, the use of behavioural assignments or other means of reinforcing counselling gains.

Do not think in terms of either formal counselling or independent self-change. Consider the many possible combinations. Just as some clients are helped best by being referred to other therapeutic arenas, so they may find it profitable to explore self-help groups such as Alcoholics Anonymous, or to attend co-counselling classes. One client who began singing classes during his time in psychotherapy realized that in fact he was soon learning much more about himself from his singing classes than from his therapy, for example. Use these ideas as a balance against the temptation to become your clients' guru, while at the same time remaining sensitive to the genuine needs of those clients who may be more fragile or slower in their learning, or who genuinely need a period of corrective emotional experience. Also, consider increasing the interval between sessions as counselling progresses, in order to encourage clients to experiment with being their own counsellor.

Key point

Do not succumb to the temptation to become indispensable to your clients, but increasingly help them to view themselves as capable of being their own counsellors.

---

25 Prepare for ending and the use of follow-up sessions

In our book *Brief Counselling* (Dryden and Feltham, 1992b) we have explored the subjects of the conscious use of time and its limits, and choices of different endings. When counselling is anticipated or agreed to be brief, then the nature of ending, its meaning and emotional impact, is likely to be quite different from counselling which has been lengthy and intimate. In cases where you have contracted to work within well-defined time limits, the end of your work together will be anticipated from the very beginning and can often be a spur to greater commitment and action. Such counselling is likely to be highly active and to include homework assignments. In addition, it is likely to encourage the generalization of learning and relapse prevention strategies. There is ample evidence that brief counselling, whether 'by default' or 'by design', is the norm rather than the exception and that many clients anticipate that they will, and prefer to, attend for a short time. This is something that you would do well to raise at the beginning of your work with clients. Where goals have been clear and concrete and are achieved in a reasonable time, there tends to be a rather natural ending. Where there has been a failure to discuss or agree on goals, or where clients have become unhealthily dependent on counselling, then ending can become problematic. Counsellors' attitudes towards the termination of counselling are also coloured by their theoretical orientation.

We suggest that you raise the subject of ending if your client does not. Do this sensitively, of course. There are clients who, because of the nature or extent of their problems or damage, require rather lengthy, non-threatening counselling which may taper off only after months and years. Even in such cases, however, it is advisable to implant the idea that the counselling relationship will not last for ever and is not an end in itself. Praise and reinforce your client's changes throughout the counselling process, remind the client of his or her original problems and goals and encourage self-counselling and generalization of learning. 'You seem to be making great headway towards resolving the concerns you came here about' is the kind of statement which honours the client's efforts and suggests that an end is in sight.

Of course, counselling does not always go as planned or as hoped. Some clients drop out 'prematurely' (before we expect them to) because they are dissatisfied, uncommitted, afraid, or because they are not getting on with you and cannot tell you, or even sometimes because they have got what they wanted, for now, and have no need of or wish for a ceremonious exit! Premature termination or ending that is not mutually agreed upon is fairly common, and all counsellors experience it. Sometimes clients wish to end before we consider they are ready. In such cases, we advocate gracefully letting go, rather than making clients feel guilty or worried. Accept the fact that endings quite often do not happen as they ideally 'should'. By this we mean that some practitioners believe that ending necessarily entails a sense of loss, separation feelings, bereavement, and so on, and that these ideally should be worked through before termination. Although we do not share this belief, we accept that it does apply to *some* clients. With those clients who have formed a therapeutically close relationship with you and who need a gradual ending in which important feelings of loss are placed in perspective, by all means address such feelings.

There are other perspectives on ending. Some counsellors regard the process of help-seeking as a cyclical one and discard the model of counselling or therapy which claims to effect a 'once and for all time' change. In other words, you may acknowledge that some clients will work on certain pressing issues now and return later, to you or to another counsellor. Another pattern of ending is the gradual tapering off of sessions (from weekly to fortnightly, to monthly, for example) reinforced by homework assignments which strengthen the clients' ability to be their own counsellor. In cognitive-analytic therapy (Ryle, 1990) active client participation is expected from the outset and the time-limited contract is concluded by a 'goodbye letter' from counsellor to client and vice versa. This enables progress to be validated, feelings to be aired, unfinished business to be expressed and future plans and needs to be formulated. Such procedures modestly and realistically acknowledge that clients may feel some disappointment that not everything can be changed. You may ask your client as you work towards termination, 'Is there anything that you haven't brought up that you'd still like to?' or 'Is there anything I could have done that would have helped you more?' Such questions should not be regarded as invitations to further, even endless, counselling, but as ways of airing feelings and sharing important information. Of course it will be helpful in certain cases to disclose intimate feelings of affection, appreciation and loss.

It is also a useful practice to consider using follow-up sessions. Your decision to schedule a follow-up session some weeks or months in the future will depend on how long, and at what intervals, you have been meeting. It has been found that this practice offers emotional containment to many clients; they know they will see you again and they are comforted by that knowledge. A follow-up meeting means that counselling is not quite over, and can feel like a safety net. In the meantime clients can continue to consolidate gains and even to increase commitment to personal change. One advantage of follow-ups is that they provide a mechanism for evaluating the endurance of therapeutic improvement. At the follow-up session, ask questions such as 'What do you remember most about our original sessions together? What do you think helped you to achieve your goals? Have you noticed any difficulties in maintaining the progress you made?' Also, don't treat this session as necessarily only a review of what has gone before. Ask clients what current problems they may be experiencing, enquire into connections between what they learned before and how they could put that learning into operation now. As Talmon (1990) has shown, a considerable amount can be achieved in a single session. This time also gives you the opportunity of checking to what extent clients really are increasingly exercising their autonomy, with your help, instead of using counselling as a retreat from responsibility.

Key point

Consider that there is a variety of ways of ending and that these may be determined partly by your initial contract; be flexible and sensitive to each client's needs in preparing for ending and organizing follow-up sessions.

V Developing Professional Knowledge and Self-reflection

26 Consider using questionnaires and inventories for clarification, catalytic and evaluation purposes

Formal assessment procedures and instruments are not popular among counsellors, particularly those counsellors who regard their work as primarily relationship-based. Dislike of and reluctance to use questionnaires and inventories may be due to a variety of factors. You may not be familiar with them, or comfortable using them. You may regard them as belonging exclusively to theoretical approaches other than your own. You may believe them to be unhelpful, unnecessary or dehumanizing. A common fear is that formal data-gathering exercises lead to clients being labelled or treated as objects or specimens of psychopathology. The idea of 'administering a psychological test' may come to mind for many counsellors, who would feel that such procedures demonstrate a 'doing to' rather than a 'being with' approach to clients. Mistrust of questionnaires is understandable, but we wish here to advocate simply that they can be useful for certain clients in certain circumstances.

Let us consider some of the kinds of questionnaires and inventories you might consider using, and what their rationales are.

Initial assessment

Whether you actually assess your clients' concerns formally at the outset or not, depends on the setting in which you work (such as clinic, community centre or college); the professional training you have had (for example, psychologist, psychotherapist or counsellor); and your predominant theoretical orientation (for example, psychodynamic, cognitive-behavioural, or person-centred). You may be compelled by the setting, or by your seniors, to use or indeed to avoid using formal assessment procedures; or these may be used before you have clients referred to you. Your training, or trainers, may have insisted on, encouraged, discouraged or forbidden the use of formal assessment procedures. Your approach to counselling may or may not lend itself obviously to the use of formal means of assessing clients.

Consider the *Psychotherapy File* of cognitive-analytic therapy (Ryle, 1990). This is a self-administered questionnaire which clients are asked to read and complete in conjunction with an explanation for its use. The psychotherapy file aims to help clients identify their own 'snags', 'traps' and 'dilemmas', or various kinds of enduringly dysfunctional attitudes. The purpose of this exercise is not to pigeon-hole the client but to identify predominant, problematic self-defeating themes. It is used and openly discussed by client and counsellor in order to formulate a working profile of the client, along with realistic therapeutic goals. Ryle contends that exercises of this kind lend structure, containment and purpose to counselling. The counselling does not become bound or inhibited by the profile, but is facilitated by it. Indeed, the client's attitude to the profile may yield significant material on which to work and it can therefore be regarded as providing 'leverage' to the counselling (Egan, 1990). Furthermore, the client's attitude towards you – the counsellor who is perceived to have suggested or 'imposed' this exercise on the client – may manifest in nuances of transference which you may choose to interpret therapeutically. As you can perhaps appreciate, the use of a formal assessment instrument can have dual functions: it invites information and may also stimulate thoughts and feelings. Use such questionnaires flexibly. With a highly reactant client (that is, a person who is highly sensitive to perceived threats to his or her autonomy) you may gain more by exploring the client's feelings about such an exercise, while with a compliant or technically-minded client, useful therapeutic information may be established.

Lazarus's (1981) *Multimodal Life History Questionnaire* is a comprehensive data-gathering instrument which asks for detailed biographical information, details of past and present psychological and physical problems, relationships and many other aspects of clients' lives. This questionnaire is designed to identify comprehensively the seven modalities – that is, behaviour, affect, sensation, imagery, cognition, interpersonal and drugs (or biological factors) – in which clients experience their problems. Multimodal therapists use such information both at the beginning of a counselling relationship and throughout it as a means of tracking each client's unique expressions of their problems and their likely remedies. Lazarus believes that such information prevents counsellors from having to grope in the dark and work haphazardly. This questionnaire guides subsequent counselling rather than limiting it to pre-ordained therapeutic plans.

Quite a different kind of questionnaire is provided by Barker et al. (reproduced in Dryden and Feltham, 1992b). The *Opinions About Psychological Problems Questionnaires* are designed to ascertain what kind of theoretical orientation may best help clients. Imagine that you have a female client whose views on her own problems fit very closely with a humanistic approach, but that you offer an entirely behavioural approach. The contrasting views of client and counsellor sometimes fail to surface, or may fortuitously lead to a productive outcome. But it can also be the case that you might have more productively identified such stark contrasts by using such questionnaires. Results which indicate that there may be a mismatch between client and counsellor, can lead you to make a referral or to adjust your approach.

If you are in doubt about how to present questionnaires to clients, consider the *Life Performance Inventory* devised by Rusk (1991). This is presented to clients at the beginning of counselling and contains standard biographical questions, as well as questions on relationships, sex, work, living conditions, health and general lifestyle. Rusk, who refers to his questionnaires and inventories as 'worksheets', does not regard them as prescriptive but as raising the client's 'evolving goals and needs'. He introduces the Life Performance Questionnaire with these words:

> 'As your consultant, I'm asking you to fill out this questionnaire. It may be a tedious job, but it will give us both a baseline from which to consider possible changes. The ultimate goal is to find ways for you to improve your well-being and satisfaction. The use of a questionnaire format for this kind of data allows us to make the best use of the valuable time we will spend on a person-to-person basis.' (Rusk, 1991: 241)

Specific problems

Scott and Stradling (1992) address the kinds of symptoms found among clients experiencing post-traumatic stress disorder. They present several examples of inventories which are designed to gather information and generate insight and problem-solving cognitions in this difficult area of counselling. Horowitz's *Impact of Event Scale* and Hammarberg's *PENN Inventory* both invite information on how clients have reacted to traumatic events in their lives. The *Trauma Belief Inventory* (Scott and Stradling, 1992) gathers information on the specific beliefs which clients entertain about themselves following a traumatic event. Now, it can be argued that all such information can be gathered just as well by other methods which do not involve questionnaires. For many clients, that is probably the case. But some clients have great difficulty relating their experiences, or organizing them, and may well benefit from these kinds of structured inventories. Exercises of this nature often have particular value when clients are confused or depressed, and the exercises can help by providing a reference point for clients who are struggling to reintegrate thoughts after a shattering experience. The exercises can also help counsellors to reflect on their clients' experiences and to consider possible therapeutic strategies.

Scott (1989) includes in his book on cognitive-behavioural therapy many examples of questionnaires and inventories which can be used to help focus clients and counsellors on clients' specific problem areas and the ways in which they may be changed. These include a *Social Questionnaire* which addresses interpersonal functioning; the *Relationship Belief Inventory* which examines some of the unhelpful cognitive patterns that clients may bring to their relationships; and the *Drug Related Attitude Questionnaire* which attempts to identify many possible reasons for harmful drug use. Let us be clear that we are not advocating that you unthinkingly reach for the apposite questionnaire every time you encounter a specific problem. Rather, consider how some of your clients may be helped to articulate their thoughts and describe their behaviour by using such questionnaires, and how you yourself may benefit from clarifying clients' underlying themes and predominant self-defeating tendencies.

Catalytic interventions

An approach to changing serious drinking problems, the '12 steps' programme of Alcoholics Anonymous, is about as far removed from 'establishment' psychology as you can get. A central feature of the 12 steps, however, requires the self-confessed alcoholic to 'make a searching and fearless moral inventory' of him or herself, which is later shared with another person. The strength of such an exercise, whatever critics may say about the religious ethos of the programme, is probably that it encourages people systematically to reflect hard on their lives in an objective fashion, which reinforces their motivation and effects the cathartic release of emotion. Encouraging clients to write their own record of their past behaviour, or even when necessary to tape-record such an inventory, stimulates active participation in counselling and promotes self-change.

Transactional analysts make a great deal of use of diagrammatic and written descriptions of clients' scripts, injunctions, drivers, rackets and games. Reality therapists use pragmatically whatever written procedures help clients to identify and begin to change dysfunctional behaviour. Glasser (1989) cites many case examples in which clients are asked to complete questionnaires which concretely identify problematic attitudes and behaviour. These are designed to challenge clients to gain new perspective on their problems, often in a fairly confrontative manner. You may feel at certain points in your counselling with particular clients that things become stuck, or a clear focus is not forthcoming. While some practitioners prefer to 'stay with' such stuckness, we suggest that you consider the advantages and disadvantages, for each of your clients, of using questionnaires in a way which may prove helpfully catalytic. In brief and time-limited counselling, such interventions are certainly to be commended, because they facilitate the highly goal-directed nature of that kind of work.

Evaluative purposes

One of the most significant features of reality therapy is its insistence that clients always make choices in their lives and are capable of making rational evaluations of those choices. In counselling underachieving schoolchildren, those with eating problems and other difficult clients, reality therapists frequently use purpose-designed questionnaires to elicit their clients' self-evaluations of current and desired behaviour (see Glasser, 1989). This kind of questionnaire enables the client to compare the likely results of present with alternative behaviour. Similar questionnaires, profiles and diagrammatic assessments of clients' target problems and their possible resolutions are used liberally in cognitive-analytic therapy. Evaluation can be done by the client alone or together with the counsellor, and can focus on past, present and future behaviour.

Questionnaires can also be used, of course, to evaluate the progress of counselling. Used at the beginning and end of counselling, evaluative questionnaires can yield important reinforcing information for the client. It is quite simple, for example, to design your own questionnaire to identify your clients' presenting problems, their frequency, duration, severity, with any accompanying thoughts and feelings. Clients may complete an initial questionnaire and compare their responses in this, towards the termination of counselling, by repeating the exercise. This can help sceptical or particularly depressed clients to gauge actual progress. You may decide to use questionnaires in the middle phase of counselling in order to review progress or impasses and to make any necessary changes in your counselling strategy. You may also wish to use questionnaires to evaluate the service you or your organization are providing. Such questionnaires may be given to clients after counselling has terminated and may include items relating to how welcoming the service was, how helpful the counsellor was, and what could have been more helpful. Counsellors may also wish to use their own case evaluation questionnaires after completing a case. For an example, see Garfield's form for this purpose (reproduced in Dryden and Feltham, 1992b).

Key point

However 'alien' to your approach to counselling, think carefully about the advantages that various kinds of questionnaires and inventories may have for certain clients at certain times.

---

27 Utilize research findings

Many counsellors dislike and disregard research in the field of counselling altogether. It is still the case that few training courses, except within academic settings, address the importance of research and the issues involved in it. This state of affairs may be partly explained by a tendency of many counsellors to have an artistic rather than a scientific bias. It may be partly due to the way in which much research is presented and the difficulty many counsellors experience in grasping its meaning. Although Rowan (1989) declares that he is not satisfied with either anecdotal evidence or 'faith' regarding whether counselling works, he is also not satisfied with most existing research methods and studies. We believe he is right to approach existing research with caution and many of the problems of research methodology and reasons for counsellors to apply research findings cautiously are put forward in Dryden (1991d).

In spite of such reservations, however, we invite you to consider what the field would look like without research. Imagine that there was no way of comparing what different counsellors were doing, how long-term counselling compared with short-term, how one orientation compared with another, how experienced practitioners compared with untrained helpers, which client problems were changed by certain methods more reliably than by others, what clients thought about their experiences of counselling, and so on. Perfectly reliable and valid ways of ascertaining such data may not yet have been found, and practitioners are certainly advised not to alter their practice on the basis of results from a few studies or a single study. However, research results are often indicative and we believe that reflective practitioners improve their work by at least considering the possible implications of counselling research.

Various research studies have been cited in this book and you may find them more or less helpful or relevant to your practice. Consider the work of Patten and Walker (1990) and Walker and Patten (1990) on couple counselling, as an example. These studies contain the reports of interviewed clients which suggest the following. More than half of those interviewed believed that 'a counsellor who was married with children would be most likely to be of help'. None of those interviewed considered that an unmarried or unpartnered counsellor would be most helpful. More than 90 per cent of those interviewed considered that it would be helpful to know their counsellors' opinions about their marriage problems. The finding was unanimous that a counsellor-provided explanation of counselling techniques would be helpful. Some of these findings may challenge your cherished therapeutic or social beliefs. What do they mean to you if you consider 'I can empathize with clients who have problems in their relationships just as well whether I am married or not', or 'According to my theoretical understanding, clients who ask for explanations are not feeling contained'? These findings in themselves may not prove or disprove anything conclusively, but they represent a challenge which we as counsellors ignore at our peril. In the latter of these research studies, where counsellors were interviewed on their beliefs, it was found, for example, that only 64 per cent considered it helpful to explain counselling techniques to their clients. What do you make of this discrepancy between client and counsellor views?

The enthusiasm counsellors bring to their work is possibly one of its most therapeutic factors. By the same token, however, some counsellors may be blindly, naively or stubbornly enthusiastic about an exclusive approach to counselling which may or may not have been exposed to rigorous research. The field of counselling is peculiarly prone to the advent of novel, 'quick-fix' (and slow-fix!) techniques, some of which are taught on weekend workshops, for example. Where do they most often get tested? Perhaps too often on unsuspecting clients on Monday mornings following the workshops! Now, enthusiasm and experimentation have their place, but so do caution, ethical considerations and quality control. Many counsellors are convinced that substantial, if not ongoing, investment in one's own therapy, is the most essential component of training and the maintenance of professional competence. There is very little research support for this proposition, however, which suggests either inadequacy in research methodology or possibly an unfounded faith in the benefits of extensive personal therapy. We realize that this is a controversial area and it is not our intention to recommend jettisoning your own personal therapy (although see our concluding remarks in Section 20 on *how* such therapy may be better utilized).

Perhaps the most compelling argument for research and its usefulness to the counsellor is embodied in the question 'How can I best help my client?' When you are confronted with a new client, whose cluster of problems includes, say, severe depression or obsessive-compulsive disorder, will you just hope for the best, applying ideas and skills with which you are familiar, or will you search out information to help you? Your supervisor may or may not have expertise in certain conditions. Examine your attitude to the concept of 'treatment (or intervention) of choice'. Do you allow for the possibility that there may be recommended interventions for certain problems, which you may or may not be able to offer? (See Section 4.) If you are interested in familiarizing yourself with major research issues and findings in counselling and psychotherapy, see Garfield and Bergin (1986). Cramer (1992) reviews some of the main personality theories used in counselling and how these measure up in the light of research. For information on counselling research methods, concepts, problems, ethics, etc., see Watkins and Schneider (1991). If you doubt that research holds any possible interest or excitement, read Norcross's very accessible account (Dryden 1991c).

Key point

Examine your attitude towards counselling research and how this may be changed if necessary. Keep abreast of research developments in the field and consider how you might use these to offer a better service to your clients.

---

28 Develop an informed and disciplined approach to eclectic and integrative practice (including when not to be eclectic)

There are many issues involved in the question of eclecticism and integration. The first is: what do they mean? Eclecticism is the pursuit and practice of the most appropriate techniques in working with different clients, while integration (or 'integrationism') is the pursuit of developing an integrated or unified approach to counselling. Eclecticism is characterized by choosing from and applying existing techniques in a pragmatic spirit, recognizing that the field of counselling has much to offer but is still relatively young and that its scientific formulations are far from satisfactory. Integration is characterized by the attempt to identify common elements in divergent models of counselling, to synthesize theories with the ultimate aim of creating a unified approach. Debates on eclecticism and integration are currently very heated in the counselling world and there is even a danger of conflicting models of these movements emerging. See Dryden (1992b) for examples of the current state of this movement in Britain.

But how does this affect you, the practitioner? It is likely that, if you have trained in Britain, you are well-grounded in one theoretical orientation. It is the position of the British Association for Counselling, as well as many trainers, that a thorough training in one core model equips you with a coherent map for understanding and working with clients. Some counsellors, by temperament or conviction, work very faithfully within a particular tradition. There is some evidence that a majority, however, are to some extent eclectic, if only in that they instinctively adapt their approach to individual clients. Most counsellors do expose themselves to developments in theory and practice which diverge from their original training and short courses offering samples of innovative techniques are well attended. We think there are two possible problems involved in training and retraining. On the one hand, blind allegiance to one model of counselling is likely to render you less effective in dealing with a wide variety of clients and client problems. On the other hand, the temptation to practise 'hat rack eclecticism' (impulsively trying out new techniques) can lead to undisciplined and ineffective counselling. Consider whether you fall into either category, and if you do, do you consider our concerns justified?

We believe that integrative practice is a life-long commitment. By exposing yourself to reading, research, continuing professional education, supervision and reflection on your work and on the counselling profession, you inevitably seek to make sense of contradictions and to hone your practice to serve each of your clients more effectively. One form of integration that has growing support is the combination of two major orientations which arguably gives practitioners a broader theoretical base and wider range of techniques. But if you are not so trained, you must obviously use what you *do* know with every client who presents themselves for counselling. Depending on your principal theoretical orientation, you may be inclined to use habitual strategies. You may, for example, always let your client take the lead, you may always foster transference, or always employ cognitive and behavioural tasks. Some counsellors are probably willing to become 'technical eclectics' (see Dryden, 1991a) in that they systematically identify each of their clients' problems, deficits and needs and, with reference to research, experience and awareness of resources offered by other professionals, apply diverse techniques or make suitable referrals.

In looking at tasks (Section 12), we have covered some of these issues previously. If you are committed to explicit discussion with your clients as to the best and mutually understood and agreed techniques, then you will inevitably be flexible. Note, again, the distinction between responsible flexibility and compulsive attraction to technical novelty! Multimodal therapy, as described by Lazarus (Lazarus, 1987; Dryden, 1991a) aims to assess clients' problems comprehensively in terms of the seven different modalities of behaviour, affect, sensation, imagery, cognition, interpersonal and biological factors. This form of technical eclecticism, far from 'doing whatever feels right', identifies and matches, as precisely as possible, each client's varying needs and available therapeutic resources. Lazarus refers to current research and is willing to utilize techniques drawn from theoretical models other than his own (originally social learning theory) if these are indicated. While Lazarus readily acknowledges that the counselling field is far from being scientifically understood and underpinned, he does not practise in a hit-or-miss manner. We advocate that you, likewise, practise in an informed and constantly evolving way, thinking hard about the advantages and otherwise of eclectic practice.

To illustrate a counter-argument to the use of tailored interventions we refer to the research of Schulte et al. (1992). Groups of phobic clients were offered individualized (tailored) therapy, standardized (manual-based) therapy, and variable standard therapy. Using a complex research design with clients reporting simple and social phobias, agoraphobia and panic disorder, the researchers found that standardized treatment obtained superior results. Admitting that these findings are so far confined to behaviour therapy, they nevertheless speculate that perhaps the avoidance of too much flexibility is sometimes advantageous. It is partly because such findings seem to go against the grain of our preferences for working intuitively and responsively to clients' uniqueness, that we need to examine such research. So when you are working with a new client who has a phobia, and after you have noted and adapted to his or her learning style, consider what degree and kind of eclecticism you might use. In such a case, you may even consider saying, 'There is some evidence that the best results with phobias are achieved by strictly observing a certain procedure', and seeing whether the client is willing to try it. Or you may, in such a case, decide in consultation with the client, to effect a referral.

Key point

Familiarize yourself with the issues of eclecticism and integration and consider how your current practice may benefit from varying your approach.

---

29   Develop your own counselling profile

Counselling is in many ways a lonely business. After your initial substantive training period you may have relatively few opportunities formally to review and evaluate your work, except with a supervisor. One way of helping yourself periodically to review your own practice is to develop a profile of how, and how well, you are working, and to use this to formulate plans for improving areas of your work which may benefit from extra attention. In Appendix 2 we set out some of the main items you may find useful in evaluating your work. We suggest that you use this table in whichever way you find most helpful, perhaps discussing it with a colleague or supervisor. You may find it useful too to consult Hill and O'Grady's (1985) list of therapist intentions; Heron (1990: 144–58) who lists unhelpful interventions; Mays and Franks's (1985) considerations on negative outcomes; and Robertiello and Schoenewolf's (1987) 'therapeutic blunders'. These may help you to decide what your particular strengths and weaknesses are.

When you have used Appendix 2, consider an action plan. Decide, for example, which areas of your practice you wish or need to improve most, and prioritize these. Which do you need to address urgently, which within the next year, and which within the next five years? Identify the best resources for such improvements (for example, supervision, personal therapy, further training, reading, peer discussion, change of job/client group, or taking a sabbatical). What will facilitate or impede your plans (including emotional resistance, cognitive obstacles, financial and other circumstances)? What is the single most important task facing you?

Key point

Systematically review your own strengths and deficits, identify areas requiring attention and establish a plan of action for improving these areas.

30 Learn to supervise yourself as well as learning from supervision from others

Counsellors are professionally obliged to receive ongoing supervision from the moment they begin working with clients. This may take the form of one-to-one supervision from an experienced practitioner, group supervision with an experienced practitioner leading or facilitating the group, peer supervision, and various permutations of the above. There are many different styles of supervision which are coloured by theoretical orientation, institutional requirements and the precise nature of the contract agreed on between supervisor and supervisee. Such supervision is of the utmost importance in promoting the professional development of counselling and in protecting the welfare of clients. However, what we think is often overlooked is the counsellor's self-supervision and his or her selective uses of supervision. In deciding to take certain cases to your supervisor, you may avoid or minimize the importance of other cases. You may be judging that certain cases are more or less worrying, or carry more or less opportunity for learning than others. For this reason among others, one of us (WD) asks his trainees on occasion to bring in all their tapes so that he can operate his 'lucky dip' technique to monitor the trainees' skill level and to discover what conscious or unconscious censorship factors may be at work.

We encourage you to think about opportunities for self-supervision in addition to mandatory supervision by others. Developing the skills needed for 'internal supervision' is, indeed, advocated by many psychodynamic therapists, most notably Casement (1985). Casement distinguishes between the counsellor's internalization of his or her actual supervisor, and the 'capacity for spontaneous reflection'. There is a danger of slipping into and being cramped by the 'borrowed thinking' of one's supervisor. It is important, within sessions, to be able to monitor rapidly and accurately one's responses and to adjust them as necessary. According to Casement, the counsellor can benefit from a somewhat playful (internal) attitude which may include avoiding preconceptions, theme abstraction, 'trial identification' (akin to empathetic approximations) and awareness of the client's sometimes codified statements which are aimed at correcting the counsellor's errors. Casement suggests that particular attention be paid to dreams, memories and stories reported by clients, in which key figures behave damagingly, clumsily or insensitively, since these may be allusions to the behaviour of the counsellor. Some clients are able to tell you directly that you are 'getting it wrong', but others are not.

So you can extend your awareness of what is happening within sessions between you and the client. But you can also learn about your own work in a variety of other ways. We believe that tape-recording is probably the most accurate and useful means. We have explained some of the ethical and technical issues involved in tape-recording elsewhere (Dryden and Feltham, 1992b). Do examine any resistance you may have to the use of tape-recording. It is often claimed that 'clients don't like/allow it' or 'it's not ethical' but these claims in practice hold little water. A majority of clients, in our experience, allow it and find no ethical problems with it. The more you record and listen to your tapes, the more likely you are to become convinced of the value of this practice. Using either something like the counsellor profile (see Appendix 2) or the Hill and O'Grady (1985) list of therapist intentions, you can profitably examine why you said certain things and not others, how facilitative or otherwise your timing and pacing is, how well you have understood your client, and so on. You can also study tapes to discover which things are left unsaid and to consider how you might have intervened differently. In addition, you can offer to give tapes to clients (as recommended by Rusk, 1991) or to listen to them with clients to enable both of you to identify and improve problem areas.

It is of course true that you can also write up and learn from process recordings of sessions, but these are less reliable than tapes. You can also devise your own method of reviewing sessions immediately after they end. Van der Veer (1992: 168) suggests that a checklist is useful, which may contain items such as how you intended to begin the session; what interventions you considered before it began; what the content of the session actually was; what your own unvoiced associations were in the session; what new information emerged; whether you adhered to certain strategies or 'deviated'; and what your intentions now are for the next session. Whichever method you do use, consider exactly which aspects of your counselling you wish to learn more about. Are there particular issues that recur and from which you seem not to be learning, for example? Is your relationship with a particular client stuck, difficult, too cosy, or collusive? Such problem areas may be identified and worked through in supervision sessions but it can do no harm, and is likely to enhance your grasp of the issue, if you find ways of supervising yourself. Let us repeat that self-supervision is not a replacement for supervision from a supervisor. Supervisors are, for example, able to confront you in a way that you may not be able to confront yourself. But they cannot monitor your moment-by-moment intentions and interactions, except in the case of live supervision. Nor can they monitor all your work with every client. You are the person 'on the spot' and you will find it helpful to adopt what Casement calls a 'supervisory viewpoint' on what you are doing.

A word of caution is in order. Do not strive to become completely independent of your supervisor, who is an ally. Do not idealize your supervisor, either. However, do not become so concerned with self-supervision that you slip into dysfunctional 'spectatoring'. As Casement puts it, 'too active a preoccupation of self-monitoring can disturb the free-floating attention' (1985). You may lose concentration on what the client is saying, but also you may become overvigilant and overconcerned about your performance. So use and develop self-supervision intelligently, without converting it into anxious perfectionism!

Key point

Think about the ways in which you can supervise yourself and add what you learn from this to the feedback your supervisor gives you.

Epilogue

We are aware that this is a short book which is attempting to cover many areas of counselling practice. It is our hope, however, that within this compact format we have been able to make some important and helpful points. If some of these key points have registered with you as indicators of what you may need to do to develop your counselling, then our goal has been met.

We hope that in some small way, at least, the points made here will combine with your own ongoing efforts to provide a better service for the clients who consult you. Feedback on this book is very welcome, especially any constructive ideas on how future editions may be improved.

May we wish you well in your counselling, at whatever stage you find yourself, and may we repeat that neither this nor any other book should become an unhelpfully injunction-like text fuelling any self-doubts you may have. Developments in counselling practice are made by conscientious, but not anxious, monitoring of your work, and also by a depth of experience which can only be gained from immersion in the counselling process.

Appendices

1 Specimen information sheet

COUNSELLOR INFORMATION

Name:

Address:

[Give directions to this address by car and public transport; information on parking, etc.]

Telephone:

[Clarify best times to call, when not to call, whether there is an answering machine, etc.]

Personal profile:

[This is optional but can include age, gender, race, languages spoken and any other information clients may find helpful in deciding whether to contact you.]

Training and qualifications:

[Include all significant training and counselling-related qualifications, accreditations, etc.]

Experience:

[Include relevant counselling-related work and voluntary experience.]

Professional activities:

[Include any supervision or training you provide; committees you have belonged to; research; publications; etc.]

Professional memberships:

[for example, BAC, BPS, BAP, etc.]

Code of Ethics:

[as above]

Supervision arrangements:

[State frequency, individual or group, etc.]

Confidentiality:

[You are advised to familiarize yourself thoroughly with the BAC (or other) Code of Ethics on confidentiality. Assure clients that your work with them is confidential except in certain instances, namely: (1) you must discuss your work with supervisors; (2) if you should have reason to think that the client is a danger to him- or herself or to others you will, after discussion with the client and preferably with his or her permission, consult with colleagues; (3) if you have reason to suspect that the client is implicated in child abuse (again, as for (2)); (4) if for any reason a Court of Law should subpoena you or seize your records, you must comply. You should also spell out the implications for confidentiality of any of your tape-recording or note-taking.]

Length and frequency of sessions and duration of counselling:

[Spell out any preferences you may have about initial assessment sessions, minimal number of 'trial' sessions for example, four, six or ten; punctuality; flexibility of scheduling; availability for short-term and long-term counselling, etc.]

Counselling theory and methods used:

[Identify and briefly describe your orientation(s) and any implications, in lay language; refer to one or two books on your orientation if helpful.]

Way of working and specialities:

[Include here your preference for making contracts regarding specific goals, for using homework assignments, review sessions, etc.; also any particular skills such as couple counselling, sex therapy, art therapy, counselling gay men, etc.]

Fees:

[Specify your hourly (or 50-minute) fee, whether there is no charge for assessment or an extra charge, whether your fees vary according to the time of day/evening, and for individuals and couples, whether you have a sliding scale, the manner in which and when you prefer payment, etc.]

Cancellation policy:

[Specify, for example, that payment in full is expected if you are given less than 24 hours notice of cancellation; and any other preferences you have.]

Other information:

[You may choose to include the names and addresses of counselling and other organizations such as BAC, MIND, Social Services, etc., locally and nationally; and also any references to literature that may help the client prepare for counselling.]

2 Counsellor profile

Ask yourself the following questions in each of these nine areas of practice. You may decide to score (for example, 1–10) or rank each item in relation to others where this is applicable. You may decide to focus on 'best' and 'worst' items. You may keep this exercise to yourself or discuss it with others. Add any items you wish.

1 *Core conditions and skills*

(a) Which of the following do I value most/least and which do I practise most/least easily and effectively?

acceptance	empathy	congruence
concreteness	immediacy	confrontation
appropriate		
self-disclosure	attending	paraphrasing
summarizing	probing	

(b) What might I do to improve any deficits here?

2 *Structuring skills*

(a) Which of the following skills do I use explicitly, clearly and often; which do I regard as implicit and seldom use?

explaining	contracting	negotiating
goalsetting	boundary-keeping	homework-setting

> developing and
> maintaining the
> reflection process   preventing relapse   terminating

(b)   How can I specifically improve my structuring?

3   Core theoretical model

(a)   How thoroughly trained and supervised am I in one central theory and its practice?
(b)   To what extent do I either explain this model to clients, or expect them not to need to know, or to find out for themselves within counselling or by reading?
(c)   Do I realize the limitations of my chosen model?
(d)   How, and to what extent, am I prepared to gain knowledge and skills in other models and to use them eclectically?

4   Use of self

(a)   How aware am I of using my own personal resources in my counselling practice?
(b)   How much value do I place on being in touch with, and using my feelings in the service of my clients?
(c)   How am I increasing my ability to use myself and to discriminate between my own and my clients' feelings in terms of the following?

warmth	voice quality	energy
creativity	intuition	assertiveness
depth of feelings	clearness of thinking	modelling
awareness of countertransference		

5   Conceptualization of client concerns

(a)   In what ways do I conceptualize client problems (for example, formally or informally, explicitly or intuitively)?
(b)   What are the strengths and weaknesses of my theoretical understanding of clients' problems?
(c)   To what extent am I willing to share and explore my clinical conjectures with clients?
(d)   How can I improve my awareness of different client problems (such as, depression, anxiety, post-traumatic stress disorder, phobias) and of possible interventions of choice?

6 Awareness and use of best resources for clients

(a) How well-informed am I about other sources of help and how willing am I to refer clients on when necessary?

(b) How familiar am I with specialist resources (for example, group therapy, free counselling services, HIV clinics) in my area?

(c) What barriers exist to improving my knowledge of the following arenas and specialist resources?

couple counselling	group therapy	family therapy
sex therapy	psychiatric treatment	medical treatment
welfare agencies	other counsellors	

7 Competence and flexibility

(a) How competent and how flexible am I in addressing issues of the following kinds: emotional issues; 'depth' (for example, regressive) issues; interpersonal issues; and cognitive/rational concerns?

(b) How competent and flexible am I regarding brief and long-term methods of counselling?

(c) How competent and flexible am I in working with specific problems (such as phobias) and with more general client agendas (such as, 'to understand myself better')?

(d) What improvements can I make in these areas and how will I make them?

8 (a) With which clients and client problems am I most successful?

People who are:

similar in temperament to me	dissimilar in temperament	same age
same/different gender	same/different race	same/different class
contemplative	active	feeling-oriented
thinking-oriented	spiritually-oriented	depressed
seriously disturbed	(add any others that you wish)	

8 (b) What can I do to improve my effectiveness with the above groups?

For both (a) and (b) examine the factors involved. Ask 'Why am I better with some people than with others? What can I learn from my strengths (to make myself even more effective) and what can I learn from my weaknesses? Am I satisfied with the current state of affairs or do I wish to improve it? If so, how?

9   Evaluation

(a)   What means am I using to monitor and evaluate my work?

supervision	tape-recording	process notes
reflection process	questionnaires	

(b)   In my counselling practice, is there a recurring or ever-present problem that I am aware of?

(c)   What do I need to do in order to improve on what I am doing well and to address those areas in which I have deficits?

References

Bennun, I. (1988) 'Systems theory and family therapy', in E. Street and W. Dryden (eds), Family Therapy in Britain. Milton Keynes: Open University Press.

Berne, E. (1970) Sex in Human Loving. New York: Simon & Schuster.

Blackburn, I.M. and Davidson, K. (1990) Cognitive Therapy for Depression and Anxiety. Oxford: Blackwell.

Bloch, S. (1990) 'Group psychotherapy', in S. Bloch (ed.), An Introduction to the Psychotherapies. Oxford: Oxford Medical Publications.

Brazelton, T.B. and Cramer, B.G. (1991) The Earliest Relationship. London: Karnac.

British Association for Counselling (BAC) (1990) Code of Ethics and Practice for Counsellors. Rugby: BAC.

Budman, S. and Gurman, A.S. (1988) Theory and Practice of Brief Therapy. New York: Guilford.

Burns, D.D. (1981) Feeling Good. New York: Signet.

Burr, V. and Butt, T. (1992) Invitation to Personal Construct Psychology. London: Whurr.

Casement, P. (1985) On Learning from the Patient. London: Tavistock.

Cramer, D. (1992) Personality and Psychotherapy. Buckingham: Open University Press.

Crowley, R.M. (1988) 'Human reactions of analysts to patients', in B. Wolstein (ed.), Essential Papers on Countertransference. New York: New York University Press.

Davanloo, H. (1990) Unlocking the Unconscious. Chichester: Wiley.

Day, R.W. and Sparacio, R.T. (1989) 'Structuring the counselling process', in W. Dryden (ed.), Key Issues for Counselling in Action. London: Sage.

De Shazer, S. (1985) Keys to Solution in Brief Therapy. New York: Norton.

Deurzen-Smith, E. van (1988) Existential Counselling in Practice. London: Sage.

Dryden, W. (1989) 'Therapeutic arenas', in W. Dryden (ed.) Individual Therapy in Britain. Milton Keynes: Open University Press.

Dryden, W. (1991a) A Dialogue with Arnold Lazarus: 'It Depends'. Buckingham: Open University Press.

Dryden, W. (1991b) Dryden on Counselling. Vol. 1: Seminal Papers. London: Whurr.

Dryden, W. (1991c) A Dialogue with John Norcross: Toward Integration. Buckingham: Open University Press.

Dryden, W. (1991d) Dryden on Counselling: Vol. 3: Training and Supervision. London: Whurr.

Dryden, W. (1992a) The Dryden Interviews: Dialogues on the Psychotherapeutic Process. London: Whurr.

Dryden, W. (1992b) Integrative and Eclectic Therapy: A Handbook. Buckingham: Open University Press.

Dryden, W. and Feltham, C. (eds) (1992a) Psychotherapy and its Discontents. Buckingham: Open University Press.

Dryden, W. and Feltham, C. (1992b) Brief Counselling: A Practical Guide for Beginning Practitioners. Buckingham: Open University Press.

Egan, G. (1990) *The Skilled Helper* (4th edn). Pacific Grove, CA: Brooks/Cole.

Ellis, A. (1985) *Overcoming Resistance: Rational-Emotive Therapy with Difficult Clients.* New York: Springer.

Fish, J.M. (1973) *Placebo Therapy.* San Francisco: Jossey-Bass.

Fransella, F. and Dalton, P. (1990) *Personal Construct Counselling in Action.* London: Sage.

Garfield, S.L. and Bergin, A.E. (eds) (1986) *Handbook of Psychotherapy and Behavior Change* (3rd edn). New York: Wiley.

Glasser, N. (ed.) (1989) *Control Theory in the Practice of Reality Therapy.* London: Harper and Row.

Goldberg, C. (1977) *Therapeutic Partnership: Ethical Concerns in Psychotherapy.* New York: Springer.

Gurman, A.S. and Kniskern, D.P. (1978) 'Research in marital and family therapy', in S.L. Garfield and A.E. Bergin (eds), *Handbook of Psychotherapy and Behavior Change* (2nd edn). New York: Wiley.

Heelas, P. (1985) 'Emotions across cultures', in S.C. Brown (ed.), *Objectivity and Cultural Divergence.* Cambridge: Cambridge University Press.

Heron, J. (1990) *Helping the Client.* London: Sage.

Hill, C.E. and O'Grady, K.E. (1985) 'List of therapist intentions illustrated in a case study and with therapists of varying theoretical orientations', *Journal of Counseling Psychology*, 32: 3–22.

Hobson, R.E. (1985) *Forms of Feeling: The Heart of Psychotherapy.* London: Tavistock.

Hodgkinson, P.E. and Stewart, M. (1991) *Coping with Catastrophe.* London: Routledge.

Holmes, J. and Lindley, R. (1989) *The Values of Psychotherapy.* Oxford: Oxford University Press.

Howard, G.S., Nance, D.W. and Myers, P. (1987) *Adaptive Counseling and Therapy.* San Francisco: Jossey-Bass.

Howe, D. (1989) *The Consumer's View of Family Therapy.* Aldershot: Gower.

Ivey, A.E., Ivey, M.B. and Simek-Downing, L. (1987) *Counseling and Psychotherapy: Integrating Skills, Theory and Practice* (2nd edn). Englewood Cliffs, NJ: Prentice-Hall.

Lazare, A. and Eisenthal, S. (1989) 'Clinical/patient relations 1: Attending to the patient's perspective', in A. Lazare (ed.), *Outpatient Psychiatry: Diagnosis and Treatment* (2nd edn). Baltimore, MA: Williams & Wilkins.

Lazarus, A.A. (1981) *The Practice of Multimodal Therapy.* New York: McGraw-Hill.

Lazarus, A.A. (1987) 'When more is better', in W. Dryden (ed.), *Key Cases in Psychotherapy.* London: Croom Helm.

Mahrer, A.R. (1989) *Experiential Psychotherapy: Basic Practices.* Ottawa: Ottawa University Press.

Maroda, K.J. (1991) *The Power of Countertransference.* Chichester: Wiley.

Mays, D.T. and Franks, C.M. (1985) *Negative Outcome in Psychotherapy and What to do About it.* New York: Springer.

Mearns, D. and Dryden, W. (eds) (1990) *Experiences of Counselling in Action.* London: Sage.

Omer, H. (1990) 'Enhancing the impact of therapeutic interventions', *American Journal of Psychotherapy*, 44 (2): 218–31.

Patten, M.I. and Walker, L.G. (1990) 'Marriage guidance counselling: 1. What clients think will help', *British Journal of Guidance and Counselling*, 18 (1): 28–39.

Pipes, R.B., Schwartz, R. and Crouch, P. (1985) 'Measuring client fears', *Journal of Consulting and Clinical Psychology*, 53 (6): 933–4.

Pitts, J.H. (1992) 'Counselor preparation: organizing a practicum and internship program in counselor education', *Counselor Education and Supervision*, 31 (4): 196–207.

Prochaska, J.O. and DiClemente, C.C. (1984) *The Transtheoretical Approach*. Homewood, IL: Dow-Jones Irwin.

Regan, A.M. and Hill, C.E. (1992) 'Investigation of what clients and counselors do not say in brief therapy', *Journal of Counseling Psychology*, 39 (2): 168–74.

Robertiello, R.C. and Schoenewolf, G. (1987) *101 Common Therapeutic Blunders*. New York: Aronson.

Rowan, J. (1989) *The Reality Game*. London: Routledge.

Rowan, J. (1990) *Subpersonalities*. London: Routledge.

Rusk, T. (1991) *Instead of Therapy*. Carson, CA: Hay House.

Ryle, A. (1990) *Cognitive-Analytic Therapy*. Chichester: Wiley.

Schulte, D., Kunzel, R., Pepping, G. and Bahrenberg-Schulte, T. (1992) 'Tailor-made versus standardised therapy of phobic patients', *Advances in Behaviour Research and Therapy*, 14: 67–92.

Scott, M.J. (1989) *A Cognitive-Behavioural Approach to Clients' Problems*. London: Tavistock/Routledge.

Scott, M.J. and Stradling, S.G. (1992) *Counselling for Post-Traumatic Stress Disorder*. London: Sage.

Simonton, O.C., Matthews-Simonton, S. and Creighton, J.L. (1988) *Getting Well Again*. London: Bantam.

Smith, D.L. (1991) *Hidden Conversations: An Introduction to Communicative Psychoanalysis*. London: Routledge.

Stewart, I. (1989) *Transactional Analysis Counselling in Action*. London: Sage.

Strean, H.S. (1959) 'The use of the patient as consultant', *Psychoanalytic Review*, 46 (2): 36–44.

Sutherland, H.J., Llewellyn-Thomas, H.A., Lockwood, G.A., Tritchler, D.L. and Till, J.E. (1989) 'Cancer patients: their desire for information and participation in treatment decisions', *Journal of the Royal Society of Medicine*, 82: 260–3.

Sutherland, S. (1992) 'What goes wrong in the care and treatment of the mentally ill', in W. Dryden and C. Feltham (eds), *Psychotherapy and its Discontents*. Buckingham: Open University Press.

Sutton, C. (1989) 'The evaluation of counselling: a goal-attainment approach', in W. Dryden (ed.), *Key Issues for Counselling in Action*. London: Sage.

Talmon, M. (1990) *Single Session Therapy*. San Francisco: Jossey-Bass.

Tannen, D. (1992) *That's Not What I Meant!* London: Virago.

Tschudi, F. (1977) 'Loaded and honest questions', in D. Bannister (ed.), *New Perspectives in Personal Construct Theory*. London: Academic Press.

VandeCreek, L. and Harrar, W. (1988) 'The legal liability of supervisors', *The Psychotherapy Bulletin*, 23 (3): 13–16.

Van der Veer, G. (1992) *Counselling and Therapy with Refugees*. Chichester: Wiley.

Wachtel, P.L. (1985) 'Integrative psychodynamic therapy', in S.J. Lynn and J.P. Garske (eds), *Contemporary Psychotherapies: Models and Methods*. Columbus, OH: Merrill.

Walker, L.G. and Patten, M.I. (1990) 'Marriage guidance counselling: II. What counsellors want to give', *British Journal of Guidance and Counselling,* 18 (3): 294-307.

Walker, M. (1990) *Women in Therapy and Counselling.* Buckingham: Open University Press.

Ware, P. (1983) 'Personality adaptations (Doors to Therapy)', *Transactional Analysis Journal,* 13 (1): 11–19.

Watkins, C.E. and Schneider, L.J. (1991) *Research in Counseling.* Hillsdale, NJ: Lawrence Erlbaum.

Winnicott, D.W. (1949) 'Hate in the countertransference', *International Journal of Psychoanalysis,* 30: 194-203.

Worden, J.W. (1991) *Grief Counselling and Grief Therapy.* London: Routledge.

Index